P9-CCT-148

Date Due

INTERACTION EFFECTS IN MULTIPLE REGRESSION

JAMES JACCARD
ROBERT TURRISI
CHOI K. WAN

Series: Quantitative Applications
in the Social Sciences

72

 a SAGE **UNIVERSITY** PAPER

SAGE **UNIVERSITY** PAPERS

Series: Quantitative Applications in the Social Sciences

Series Editor: **Michael S. Lewis-Beck,** *University of Iowa*

Publisher

Sara Miller McCune, Sage Publications, Inc.

Series / Number 07-072

INTERACTION EFFECTS
IN MULTIPLE REGRESSION

JAMES JACCARD
University at Albany

ROBERT TURRISI
University at Albany

CHOI K. WAN
University at Albany

SAGE PUBLICATIONS
The International Professional Publishers
Newbury Park   London   New Delhi

For information address:

SAGE Publications, Inc.
2111 West Hillcrest Drive
Newbury Park, California 91320

SAGE Publications Ltd.
28 Banner Street
London EC1Y 8QE
England

SAGE Publications Pvt. Ltd.
M-32 Market
Greater Kailash I
New Delhi 110 048 India

Printed in the United States of America

Library of Congress Cataloging-in-Publication Data

Jaccard, James.
    Interaction effects in multiple regression / James Jaccard, Robert
Turrisi, Choi K. Wan.
        p.   cm. — (Sage university papers. Quantitative applications
in the social sciences ; 72)
    Includes bibliographical references.
    ISBN 0-8039-3703-2
    1. Regression analysis. 2. Social sciences — Statistical methods.
I. Turrisi, Robert.   II. Wan, Choi K.   III. Title. Iv. Series: Sage
university papers series. Quantitative applications in the social
sciences ; no. 72.
HA31.3.J33   1990
519.5'36'0243 — dc20   89-10764
                                                                  CIP

FIRST PRINTING, 1990

When citing a university paper, please use the proper form. Remember to cite the current Sage University Paper series title and include the paper number. One of the following formats can be adapted (depending on the style manual used):

(1) DUNTEMAN, GEORGE H. (1989) "Principal Components Analysis." Sage University Paper series on Quantitative Applications in the Social Sciences, 07-069. Newbury Park, CA: Sage.

OR

(2) Dunteman, George H. 1989. Principal Components Analysis.Sage University Paper series on Quantitative Applications in the Social Sciences, series no. 07-069. Newbury Park, CA: Sage.

CONTENTS

Series Editor's Introduction 5

1. Introduction 7
    The Analysis of Interaction Effects 8
    A Review of Multiple Regression 15
    Terminology 19
    Overview of Book 19

2. Traditional Product Term Analysis 20
    The Form of the Interaction 22
    The Test for the Presence of an Interaction Effect 24
    The Strength of the Effect 24
    The Nature of the Effect 25
    The Interpretation of Regression Coefficients 26
    Simple Effects and "Interaction Comparison"
        Analysis of Regression Coefficients 27
    Levels of Measurement 28
    Simple Transformations and Multicollinearity 30
    A Numerical Example 31

3. Additional Issues with Traditional Product Term Analysis 33
    Standardized Solutions 33
    The Interpretation of Main Effects
        in the Presence of a Significant Interaction 34
    Power Analysis for Interaction Terms 35
    Structural Equation Models 36
    The Problem of Measurement Error 38
    Interaction with Three Continuous Independent Variables 40
    The Case of a Qualitative Moderator and a
        Continuous Independent Variable 42
    Alternative Approaches to Product-Term Analysis 48

4. More Complex Interactions 50
    Nonlinear Relationships in
        Multiple Regression: A Review 50
    Effects as a Quadratic Function of a
        Moderator Variable 55

Nonlinear Relationships and
   Interaction Analysis 59
Model Specification of
   Complex Interactions 62
Interaction Analysis of
   Complex Causal Models 63
Exploratory Analyses 64

5. Moderator Analysis of Correlation Coefficients 65
Correlations versus Slopes 66
Analysis of the Difference Between
   Independent Correlations 68
Analysis of Correlations Using the
   General Linear Model 70
Analysis of the Difference Between
   Dependent Correlations 72

6. Methodological and Substantive Issues 72
"False" Interaction Effects 73
Failure To Detect Interaction Effects 74
Ordinal and Disordinal Interactions 75
Concluding Comments 78

Appendix A
Computation of Standard Errors 80

Appendix B
Computer Programs 81
BASIC Code 83

Notes 89

References 90

About the Authors 95

SERIES EDITOR'S INTRODUCTION

In multiple regression analysis, model specification usually follows the linear additive form, such as:

$$Y = a + b_1X_1 + b_1X_2 + e$$

implying that X_1 and X_2 have independent effects, which need to be added together to predict Y. But, this specification is incorrect if the effect of X_1, say, depends on X_2. Then, a nonadditive form seems preferred, such as:

$$Y = a + b_1X_1 + b_2X_2 + b_3X_1X_2 + e$$

The multiplicative term, X_1 *times* X_2, is a new variable representing the dependency of X_1 on X_2. The slope, b_3, aims to measure this *interaction effect*.

Take an example. Suppose a student of administrative behavior, Sally Jones, contends that program innovation (I) is a function of available resources (R) and decentralized decisionmaking (D). She assumes the two variables, R and D, each contribute something on their own. She is also sure that the effect of decentralized decisionmaking is greater, at higher levels of resources. Here is the suggested regression model, with ordinary least squares estimates using centered measures.

$$I = 6.3 + 47.2*R + 36.3*D + 4.7*RD + e$$

$$R^2 = .73 \quad N = 58$$

where I is a quantitative measure of program innovation, R is a quantitative measure of resources available; D is a quantitative measure of decentralized decisionmaking; RD is a new variable, R multipled by D; * indicates statistical significance at .05; and N = a random sample of 58 administrative bureaus.

These results imply that her hypotheses are correct. R and D, by themselves, have significant main effects (b_1 and b_2). Also, the interaction effect is statistically significant (see b_3), indicating that decentralization makes an additional contribution to innovation as the value of available resources increases.

Professor Jaccard and his colleagues spell out the procedures for incorporating interactions into a multiple regression context. Starting with the simple two-way interaction, illustrated above, they move on to more complex forms, for example, three-way interactions, quadratic functions, and other nonlinear relationships. Further, they tackle nagging issues, such as measurement error, qualitative moderator variables, interpretation of main effects, and disordinal interactions. Their discussion of the endemic multicollinearity problem, with "centering" as a possible solution, is noteworthy. Throughout, the authors teach by example, drawing from sociology, psychology, and political science. Their monograph is especially valuable, given that interactions are almost certainly widespread, but appear to be little investigated in the literature.

— Michael S. Lewis-Beck
Series Editor

INTERACTION EFFECTS IN MULTIPLE REGRESSION

JAMES JACCARD
University at Albany

ROBERT TURRISI
University at Albany

CHOI K. WAN
University at Albany

1. INTRODUCTION

A large number of theoretical frameworks in the social sciences are concerned with causal models. These models focus on specifying the effects of one or more independent variables on one or more dependent variables. At the simplest level, there are six types of relationships that can occur within a causal model, as illustrated in Figure 1.1. A *direct* causal relationship is one in which a variable, X, is a direct cause of another variable, Y (i.e., it is the immediate determinant of Y within the context of the theoretical system). An *indirect* causal relationship is one in which X exerts a causal impact on Y, but only through its impact on a third variable, Z. A *spurious* relationship is one in which X and Y are related, but only because of a common cause, Z. There is no formal causal link between X and Y. A *bidirectional* or *reciprocal* causal relationship is one in which X has a causal influence on Y, which, in turn, has a causal impact on X. An *unanalyzed* relationship is one in which X and Y are related, but the source of the relationship is unspecified. Finally, a *moderated* causal relationship is one in which the relationship between X and Y is moderated by a third variable, Z. In other words, the nature of the relationship between X and Y varies, depending on the value of Z.

This monograph is concerned primarily with the statistical analysis of moderated relationships, or as they are more commonly known, interaction effects, where all variables involved are continuous in nature. The focus is on analyzing interaction effects in the context of multiple regression and structural equation analyses. There currently exists a great deal of confusion about the analysis of moderated relationships involving continuous variables. The statistical and sub-

AUTHORS' NOTE: *We would like to thank the following individuals for their comments on previous portions of this manuscript: Richard Alba, John Aldrich, George Alliger, Jacob Cohen, Bill Dillon, Ajith Kumar, and Scott Maxwell. We would especially like to thank Michael Lewis-Beck for his expert advice and support. Dr. Jaccard's contribution to this project was facilitated by grants from the Center for Population Research, National Institute of Health. Dr. Turrisi's and Dr. Wan's contributions were facilitated by a grant from the National Institute of Alcohol and Alcohol Abuse.*

7

stantive literatures are replete with contradictory advice and admonitions about the best way to test models involving moderated relationships. Further, the relevant statistical literature is scattered throughout a range of disciplines, including sociology, psychology, political science, economics, biology, and statistics, to name only a few. The major purpose of this monograph is to bring together this rather diverse literature and to explicate the central issues involved in conducting analyses of moderated relationships involving continuous variables. Our goal is to present a readable and practical introduction for the social science researcher who has working knowledge of multiple regression and structural equation models.

It is our belief that interaction effects have received somewhat short shrift in disciplines where such relationships are likely to be the rule rather than the exception. In the substantive sociological literature, for example, one readily finds formal tests of structural equation models involving direct, indirect, spurious, bidirectional, and unanalyzed relationships. However, the inclusion of interaction effects in such models is rare. A review of seven major journals in sociology and psychology (*American Journal of Sociology, American Sociological Review, Social Forces, Journal of Personality and Social Psychology, Journal of Applied Social Psychology, Journal of Experimental Social Psychology, Journal of Applied Psychology*) over the past five years yielded 116 articles that formally evaluated one or more structural equation models. Of these, only 8 included interaction effects between the endogenous variables. It indeed may be the case that interaction effects are not theoretically appropriate in any of the diverse domains in which they were ignored by these researchers. However, we suspect not. In fact, we were struck by the number of articles in which we judged interaction effects among the endogenous variables to be highly plausible. Although one could speculate on why interaction effects are infrequent in social-psychological models of human behavior, we believe that one (unfortunate) reason is the somewhat inaccessible nature of the statistical literature on this important topic. We hope that this monograph will encourage researchers to think about the possibility of interaction effects within their theoretical frameworks, and to pursue the analysis of such relationships, if it is substantively warranted.

In this chapter, we briefly review the concept of interaction effects as used in social science research. We begin by discussing the topic of interaction effects in traditional analysis of variance frameworks. We demonstrate that the concept of statistical interaction is closely tied to the notion of moderated relationships. After establishing the basic methods of interaction analysis in analysis of variance, we discuss the concept of a moderated relationship in correlational terms. Finally, we review basic multiple regression procedures, to provide a framework for future chapters.

The Analysis of Interaction Effects

Analysis of Variance Perspectives. Moderated relationships are reflected in the concept of statistical interaction, a concept that is prevalent in analysis of variance (ANOVA) paradigms. Consider the following example. A social scientist

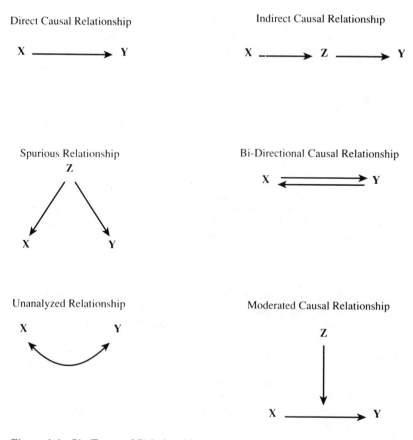

Figure 1.1. Six Types of Relationships

identifies 300 married individuals, half of whom are religious and half of whom are not religious. One-third of the individuals are Catholic, one-third are Protestant, and one-third are Jewish. This yields a 2 × 3 factorial design (religiosity by religion), with a sample size of 50 per group. The researcher is interested in how religion and religiosity are related to the number of children that the individual wants in his or her completed family. She therefore conducts a 2 × 3 analysis of variance on this dependent variable. Table 1.1 presents the mean scores that were observed, as well as a summary table for the analysis of variance. There was a statistically significant interaction effect. To specify the nature of the interaction, one of the independent variables is deemed the moderator variable (i.e., the variable that moderates the relationship between the other independent variable and the dependent variable). This designation is typically made on the basis of substantive concerns. Let religiosity be the moderator variable. The implication of the interaction effect is that the relationship between religion and desired family

TABLE 1.1

Summary Table and Means for Example of the Effects of
Religion and Religiosity on Desired Family Size

Source	Sum of Squares	df	Mean Square	F
Religion (A)	24.52	2	12.26	6.13
Religiosity (B)	19.22	1	19.22	9.61
A × B	32.77	2	16.39	8.20
Error	588.00	294	2.00	
Total	664.51	299		

	Means			
	Catholic	Protestant	Jewish	Marginal
Religious	3.15	2.45	1.81	2.47
Not Religious	1.87	1.84	1.81	1.84
Marginal	2.51	2.14	1.81	2.16

size differs, depending on whether or not the individuals are religious. It can be seen in Table 1.1 that, for religious individuals, Catholics tend to desire more children, on the average, than do Protestants, who, in turn, tend to desire more children than do Jews. This is not true, however, for nonreligious individuals. For nonreligious individuals, the average number of desired children is approximately the same in all three religious groups. Stated in more global terms, an interaction between religion and desired family size was observed, with religiosity serving as the moderator variable.

Three fundamental issues confront the social science researcher when evaluating a moderated relationship (or, for that matter, any type of the six relationships mentioned earlier): (1) Based on sample data, can we infer that an interaction effect exists in the population, (2) if so, what is the strength of the effect, and (3) if so, what is the nature of the effect? Procedures have been developed in standard analysis of variance paradigms to address each of these issues, and it will be useful to review these procedures briefly. We will refer to the data in Table 1.1 to illustrate the issues with a concrete example.

The first question (Does an interaction effect exist in the population?) is addressed by means of the traditional F test of the interaction term in the summary table. A statistically significant F leads to the conclusion that an interaction effect does, indeed, exist (within the constraints of a Type I error). A statistically nonsignificant F leads to the conclusion that an interaction effect cannot, with confidence, be said to be present. In the current example, $F(2,294) = 8.20$ and $p < 0.05$, hence we conclude that an interaction effect is present.

The second question (What is the strength of the effect?) is addressed by computing one or more indices of effect size. The choice of an effect size index is somewhat controversial. One index is *eta squared*, which is the proportion of variance in the dependent variable that is attributable to the interaction effect *in the sample data*. It is defined as:

$$\text{Eta}^2 = \frac{\text{SS}(A \times B)}{\text{SS}(T)} \qquad [1.1]$$

where SS(A × B) is the sum of squares for the interaction term, and SS(T) is the sum of squares total. In the present example, $\text{Eta}^2 = 32.77/664.51 = 0.049$. When multiplied by 100, eta squared reflects the percentage of variance in the dependent variable that is accounted for by the interaction effect in the sample data.

One problem with eta squared is that it is a positively biased estimator of the effect size in the population. Some statisticians have suggested a correction factor to adjust for this bias. One popular correction yields an index called "omega squared," which has been used as an approximately unbiased estimate of the proportion of explained variance in the population (for relevant formulas, see Hays, 1983). Unfortunately, the use of unbiased estimators also presents problems. To illustrate, consider the case where the true effect size (i.e., proportion of explained variance) in a population is small (say, equal to 0.03). When random samples of a given size (e.g., $N = 50$) are obtained and an unbiased estimator is computed, cases will arise where the value of the index is negative. This is troublesome because it is impossible, in principle, for a proportion to be negative. One would be hard-pressed to use a negative value as one's "best guess" about the true population effect size because, obviously, a value of zero would provide a "better guess" than the negative value. But if one adopts the practice of setting negative estimates to zero, then the statistic no longer is unbiased. Rather it is positively biased, much like eta squared.

Another factor to consider when selecting an index of effect size is the standard error of the index, or the extent to which the value of the index fluctuates from one random sample to another random sample of the same population. Studies have evaluated the behavior of a number of indices in this regard, and most have found eta squared to be superior. For example, in a Monte Carlo simulation, Keselman (1975) found that the bias of eta squared was minimal for small to moderate effect sizes, and that the standard error of eta squared was superior to that of omega squared. The issue of choosing an index of effect size is well beyond consideration of the present monograph. For pedagogical reasons, as well as those reasons noted above, we will adopt indices based on eta squared (or its analog in correlational data, r^2).

Methods for answering the third question (What is the nature of the interaction effect?) also are controversial in traditional ANOVA designs. At least three methods have been proposed for determining the nature of an interaction effect: (1) simple main effects analysis, (2) interaction comparisons, and (3) interaction contrasts. We will discuss each, in turn.

Consider the example about the effects of religion and religiosity on desired family size, where religiosity is designated as the moderator variable. In simple main effects analysis, the researcher conducts a separate one-way analysis of variance of the effects of religion on desired family size at each level of the moderator variable. The only deviation from standard ANOVA techniques is that the error term from the full 2 × 3 factorial analysis is used in place of the error term from the one-way ANOVAs (see Keppel, 1982). In the current example, a one-way analysis of variance of the effects of religion on desired family size yielded a statistically significant F for religious individuals ($F[2,294] = 11.23$, $p < 0.05$), but not for nonreligious individuals ($F[2,294] = 0.02$, n.s.). The statistically significant effect for religious individuals is then further analyzed by means of a post-hoc pairwise comparison procedure, such as Tukey's HSD method (see Jaccard, Becker, and Wood, 1984). This analysis reveals that all three religious groups differ significantly from each other in terms of their mean desired number of children. The nature of the interaction is thus revealed: For religious individuals, we can conclude that there is a relationship between religion and desired family size, such that Catholics want more children than Protestants who, in turn, want more children than Jews. However, for nonreligious individuals no conclusion for a relationship is warranted. The relationship between religion and desired family size differs as a function of the religiosity of the individual.

Simple main effects analysis has been criticized by several statisticians as not being an adequate diagnostic tool for discerning the nature of interaction effects (e.g., Marascuilo and Levin, 1976). Some of the problems with the approach can be illustrated by assuming that the pattern of means in Table 1.2 had been observed instead of the pattern of means in Table 1.1. For nonreligious individuals there is a relationship between religion and desired family size: Catholics tend to want more children than Protestants who, in turn, tend to want more children than Jews. This is also true for religious individuals. However, notice that the effect of religion on desired family size is more pronounced for religious individuals than for nonreligious individuals, at least when Protestants are compared to Jews. The relationship between religion and desired family size differs as a function of religiosity, with the relationship being stronger for religious individuals than for nonreligious individuals. This suggests the presence of statistical interaction, and a 2 × 3 ANOVA would yield a significant interaction effect (assuming an error term similar to that in Table 1.1).

Now suppose the investigator performed a simple main effects analysis on the data to discern the nature of the interaction effect. The separate one-way ANOVA of religion on desired family size would yield a statistically significant effect for religious individuals as well as for nonreligious individuals. Post-hoc pairwise comparisons of means would also reveal that all comparisons are statistically significant. The investigator is left with the conclusion that Catholics want more children than Protestants (on the average) who, in turn, want more children than Jews, and that this is true both for religious and for non- religious individuals. The investigator thus gains little insight into the nature or source of the interaction effect. He or she knows that *something* is different in the relationship between religion and desired family size for religious as compared to nonreligious individuals because the overall interaction effect was statistically significant. But the simple main effects analysis does not reveal the source of this difference.

As an alternative to simple main effects analysis, some statisticians have suggested the use of an approach called *interaction comparisons*. In the current example, this involves forming all possible 2 × 2 sub- tables from the original 2

TABLE 1.2

Mean Desired Number of Children as a Function of
Religion and Religiosity: Example 2

	Catholic	Protestant	Jewish	Marginal
Religous	4.15	3.65	2.23	3.34
Not Religious	3.15	2.65	1.73	2.51
Marginal	3.65	3.15	1.98	2.92

× 3 factorial design. A separate 2 × 2 ANOVA would then be conducted on each subdesign, but using the error term from the overall analysis in the formation of each F ratio. For a 2 × 3 design, there are three 2 × 2 subtables, and these are presented in Table 1.3. The major focus of interpretation is the interaction effects in each of the 2 × 2 subanalyses. For the first subtable in Table 1.3, the 2 × 2 interaction was statistically nonsignificant. This interaction tests whether the size of the mean difference between Catholics and Protestants for religious individuals is significantly different from the size of the corresponding difference for nonreligious individuals; that is, is the relationship different for religious individuals as compared with nonreligious individuals? The nonsignificant difference indicates that no such conclusion is warranted. In contrast, the 2 × 2 interaction *is* statistically significant for the second subtable. This suggests that the mean difference between Catholics and Jews is different for religious individuals as compared with nonreligious individuals. Inspection of the relevant means indicates that the differences between the Catholics and Jews is more pronounced for religious individuals than it is for nonreligious individuals. A source of the interaction effect is thus apparent. The third 2 × 2 subtable also reveals a statistically significant interaction, and indicates that the difference between Protestants and Jews also is larger for religious as opposed to nonreligious individuals. Again, this represents a source of the interaction effect.

There are many issues that must be considered when conducting interaction comparisons, especially for more complicated factorial designs. For example, given that three separate 2 × 2 analyses were performed, some control for experimentwise error rates must be introduced (e.g., via a Benferroni method, see Holland and Copenhaver, 1988, or via a Scheffe-like method, see Boik, 1979). Consideration of these issues is beyond the scope of this monograph and interested readers are referred to Boik (1979) and Keppel (1982).

Which procedure, simple main effects analysis or interaction comparisons, is preferred? The answer to this question is complex and controversial. There are cases where simple main effects analysis will adequately reveal the nature of an interaction effect, and hence it can be useful. However, there are also situations where simple main effects analysis will fail to be informative and, in fact, it can even be misleading. This will usually (but not always) be the case when there are strong main effects for the independent variables. In these instances, interaction comparisons usually will be more informative. The choice of a method is ultimately dictated by the substantive questions of the researcher and how these

TABLE 1.3

2 × 2 Subtables for Example of the Effects of
Religion and Religiosity on Desired Family Size

	Subtable 1		Subtable 2		Subtable 3	
	Catholic	Protestant	Catholic	Jewish	Protestant	Jewish
Religious	4.15	3.65	4.15	2.23	3.65	2.63
Not Religious	3.15	2.65	3.15	1.73	2.65	1.73

questions map onto the underlying statistical model. For this reason, we will develop both methods for decomposing the nature of a moderated relationship.

The third procedure for exploring interaction effects is called *interaction contrasts*. This method is similar to that of interaction comparisons. However, in this approach the subtables are defined in such a way as to yield orthogonal, single degree of freedom, contrasts that correspond to components of the overall interaction effect. This approach obviously is useful only if the contrasts make substantive sense and yield insights into the phenomenon under study. In practice, it is not common for questions of theoretical interest to map perfectly onto a set of orthogonal contrasts, although it is possible to use this strategy to good effect.

In sum, the analysis of interaction effects involves three fundamental questions: Does an interaction effect (i.e., moderated relationship) exist, what is the strength of the effect, and what is the nature of the effect? The first question is addressed through significance tests of an overall interaction term. The second question is addressed by examination of an effect size index, such as eta squared. The third question is addressed by means of simple main effects analysis, interaction comparisons, and/or interaction contrasts. Our discussion of the analysis of interaction effects involving continuous variables using multiple regression paradigms will draw parallels to each of these approaches traditionally used in ANOVA.

The Interpretation of Main Effects in the Presence of Statistical Interactions. Some statisticians (e.g., Hays, 1983) argue that it is inappropriate to interpret main effects in the presence of a statistically significant interaction effect. According to this perspective, a main effect assesses a *constant* effect of an independent variable on a dependent variable that generalizes across all levels of the moderator variable. A statistically significant interaction effect indicates that no such constant effect occurs (i.e., that the effect of the independent variable on the dependent variable is conditional on the value of the moderator variable), and hence the main effect is meaningless. In contrast, other statisticians (e.g., Overall, Lee, and Hornik, 1981) argue that main effects are meaningful in the presence of significant interactions. These researchers interpret main effects, not in terms of constant effects, but rather in terms of the *average* effect of an independent variable on a dependent variable across values of the moderator variable. These two interpretations of main effects are distinct and both have merit (see Cramer and Applebaum, 1980). In our opinion, the average effect of an independent variable on a dependent variable usually (but not always) will be a meaningful piece of information. For example, consider the data in Table 1.4. In these data, religious individuals desire, on the average, more children than nonreligious individuals. This relationship is stronger for Catholics than for Protestants, hence the presence of an interaction effect. However, the fact that an interaction is present does not diminish the utility of the information that there are sizable religious versus nonreligious differences at all levels of religion. To ignore this information and to focus solely on the conclusion that the effect is stronger in one group than the other would yield a less-than-complete picture.

Correlational Perspectives on Moderated Relationships/Interaction Effects. From the perspective of correlational statistics, moderated relationships have been analyzed in the literature using two types of parameters, correlations and slopes. In the case of the former, the question of interest is whether the correlation between two variables varies as a function of the moderator variable. In the case of the latter, the question of interest is whether the slope of the dependent variable on the independent variable differs as a function of the moderator variable. These are quite different questions because the slope is influenced not only by the correlation between the dependent variable and the independent variable, but also by the standard deviations of the variables.

There is controversy about which parameter is best suited for moderator analysis. Our discussion in the next three chapters focuses on differences in slopes as the essence of a moderated relationship. In Chapter 5, we discuss statistical methods for the moderated analysis of correlations and directly address the issue of when an investigator would be interested in correlations as opposed to slopes.

A Review of Multiple Regression

The present section assumes that the reader is familiar with the basics of fixed-effects multiple regression. The intent is to introduce terminology and a frame of reference from which future discussions will follow. For useful introductions to multiple regression, see Berry and Feldman (1985), Cohen and Cohen (1983), Lewis-Beck (1980), Pedhazur (1982), or Schroeder, Sjoquist, & Stephan (1986).

Consider the case of three continuous variables, where the investigator is interested in the effects of two independent variables X_1 and X_2 on a dependent variable (Y). The test of a simple additive (or "main effects") model for predicting Y from X_1 and X_2 typically takes the form of a sample-based least squares regression equation such that:

$$Y = a + b_1 X_1 + b_2 X_2 + e \qquad [1.2]$$

where a is the least squares estimate of the intercept; b_1 and b_2 are the least squares estimates of the population regression coefficients for X_1 and X_2, respectively, and e is a residual term. In this model, several assumptions are necessary with regard to the structure of the population data in order to apply ordinary least squares (OLS) analysis: (1) The expected value of the residual term is zero; (2)

TABLE 1.4

Example of the Effects of
Religion and Religiosity on Desired Family Size

	Catholic	Protestant
Religous	4.50	3.00
Not Religious	2.50	1.50

there is no serial correlation between residuals; (3) the residuals exhibit constant variance (homoscedasticity) across values of X; (4) the covariance between the X's and the residual term is zero; and (5) the rank of the sample data matrix equals the number of columns, and is less than the number of observations (i.e., there is not complete multicollinearity). When these assumptions are statisfied, an OLS estimator is said to be the best linear, unbiased estimator (BLUE) in that it is linear, unbiased, and has minimum variance in the class of all linear unbiased estimators.

The sample multiple correlation coefficient, R, is an index of overall model fit (in the sample), and the regression coefficients represent estimates of the "effects" of an X variable on Y, partialling out all other X variables. Specifically, a given b_i represents the number of units that Y is predicted to change given a one-unit increase in X, "holding all other X constant." If all variables are standardized, then the intercept will always equal zero and the b_i will represent *standardized* regression coefficients. Their interpretation is similar to the original *unstandardized* regression coefficients, except that all units are expressed in terms of standard scores. Thus a b_i value of 1.5 for X_1 using standardized scores implies that for every one standard score that X_1 increases, y is predicted to change 1.5 standard scores. Some social scientists prefer the use of standardized scores to unstandardized scores in multiple regression analysis, because all of the variables possess a common metric and it is supposedly easier to make substantive comparisons regarding the magnitude of the coefficients for different independent variables. We will discuss the issue in more detail in chapter 5.

Consider the following example: a sociologist is interested in the extent to which overall satisfaction with one's marital relationship could be predicted from satisfaction or dissatisfaction with six distinct components of the relationship. Three hundred thirty-nine individuals rate how satisfied or dissatisfied they are with their overall marital relationship, using an 11-point, −5 to + 5, rating scale ranging from very dissatisfied to very satisfied (with higher numbers indicating greater satisfaction). In addition, the individuals rate (on an identical scale) how satisfied they are with the following six aspects of their relationships: the amount of communication, the way affection is expressed, the amount of emotional support, the level of shared interests, the amount of time spent together, and the way conflict is resolved. The investigator performs a multiple regression analysis in which overall marital satisfaction is regressed onto the six components.

TABLE 1.5
Abbreviated SPSS Printout for Multiple Regression Example

			df	Sum of Squares	Mean Square
Multiple R	.814	Regression	6	357.897	59.650
R^2	.663	Residual	332	182.191	0.549
		F = 108.698		Signif F = 0.000	

Variable	b	SE b	Beta	SE Beta	Correl	Part Cor	T	Sig T
Conflict	.121	.025	.191	.039	.578	.155	4.88	.000
Time Together	.005	.023	.008	.038	.353	.007	.22	.823
Affection	.151	.039	.173	.044	.629	.210	3.91	.000
Share Interest	.153	.034	.183	.041	.550	.142	4.46	.000
Communication	.125	.037	.147	.044	.625	.106	3.33	.001
Emot. Support	.307	.041	.350	.046	.724	.241	7.56	.000
(Constant)	1.010	.127					7.98	.000

Table 1.5 presents the results of the analysis, using abbreviated versions of a computer printout from an SPSS-X run.

The squared multiple correlation was 0.663, which indicates the proportion of variance in the ratings of overall marital satisfaction that could be accounted for by the linear combination of the six component parts. The null hypothesis that the population multiple correlation equals zero is tested by means of an F test, reported underneath the summary table. The F is statistically significant ($F[6,332]$ = 108.698), leading us to reject the null hypothesis.

The standardized and unstandardized regression coefficients are presented in the lower half of Table 1.5. As noted above, a given unstandardized coefficient reflects the number of units that overall satisfaction is predicted to change given a one-unit change in the X variable in question, holding all other X variables constant. For example, for every one rating scale unit that satisfaction with the amount of emotional support changes, the overall satisfaction with the marital relationship is predicted to change 0.307 rating scale units (holding all other satisfaction variables constant). By contrast, a one-unit change in satisfaction with the amount of time spent together is associated with only a 0.005 unit predicted increase in overall satisfaction (holding all other components constant). The standardized coefficients are subject to the same form of interpretation, but in terms of standard scores rather than raw scores.

Each regression coefficient has associated with it an estimated standard error (see columns labeled "SE b" and "SE Beta"). These statistics represent estimates of how much sampling error is operating when estimating the regression coefficients in the population. More specifically, the estimated standard error indicates (roughly speaking) the average deviation of a sample estimate from the true value of the population parameter across all possible random samples of size N. The larger the standard error, the greater the amount of sampling error (everything else being equal), and the less confidence we have in the accuracy of the sample estimate.

The column labeled "T" indicates the t test for the null hypothesis that a given regression coefficient equals zero. The value of t equals the value of the regression coefficient divided by its standard error. The column labeled "Sig T" presents the p value for the t statistic. In this example, all the regression coefficients are statistically significant except the one associated with satisfaction about the time spent together.

Finally, additional insights into the relationship of each predictor to the criterion can be gained by examination of the zero-order correlations between each predictor and the criterion (see column labeled "Correl"), and the semipartial correlations between a given predictor and the criterion with all remaining predictors partialled out of the predictor (see column labeled "Part Cor"). The former statistic, when squared, reflects the proportion of explained variance in overall marital satisfaction that is accounted for by a given component when all other components of satisfaction are free to vary. The latter statistic, when squared, indicates the proportion of variance in overall marital satisfaction that is *uniquely* associated with a given component of satisfaction beyond all other components. For example, satisfaction with emotional support accounts for $(100)(0.72)(0.72) = 51.5\%$ of the variance in overall marital satisfaction. This component uniquely accounts for $(100)(0.24)(0.24) = 5.8\%$ of the variance in overall marital satisfaction, over and above that which is accounted for by the other five predictors in the model.[1] All of these statistics (the regression coefficients, the zero-order correlations, and the semipartial correlations) provide perspectives on the relative "importance" of predictors in determining a criterion (see Darlington, 1968, and Gordon, 1968, for elaboration).

Often, researchers perform hierarchical multiple regression tests. In these cases, the investigator is interested in whether adding one or more predictor variables to an existing multiple regression equation will significantly increase the predictability of the criterion. The incremental explained variance is typically evaluated by subtracting the squared multiple correlation in the original equation from the squared multiple correlation in the expanded equation. For example, if this difference equals 0.10, then an additional 10% of explained variance in the criterion has resulted by the inclusion of the additional predictors. A test of the null hypothesis that this increment is zero in the population is yielded by the following equation:

$$F = \frac{(R_2^2 - R_1^2)/(k_2 - k_1)}{(1 - R_2^2)/(N - k_2 - 1)} \qquad [1.3]$$

where R_2 is the multiple R for the expanded equation, R_1 is the multiple R for the original equation, k_2 is the number of predictors in the expanded equation, k_1 is the number of predictors in the original equation, and N is the total sample size. The resulting F is distributed with $k_2 - k_1$ and $N - k_2 - 1$ degrees of freedom.

Terminology

Before embarking on the formal analysis of moderated relationships, some clarifications about terminology are necessary. We frequently will make reference to variables as being "independent variables" and "dependent variables." Social scientists are in general agreement about the definition of a dependent variable. However, the term *independent variable* has assumed different meanings in various areas of the social sciences. Some investigators restrict the definition of an independent variable to a variable that is explicitly manipulated in the context of an experiment. We will adopt a more general definition of an independent variable, namely that it is a presumed cause of the dependent variable. It is not necessary for a variable to be experimentally manipulated in order that it be conceptualized as an independent variable. Rather, if a variable is presumed to cause another variable, then the presumed cause is the independent variable and the consequence of that cause is the dependent variable. Note that just because an investigator presumes that one variable causes another does not mean that the one variable does, in fact, cause the other variable. This is only a presumption made by the researcher for purposes of the investigation. Although we will adopt causal terminology in this monograph, the basic ideas that we develop do not require causal assumptions. The thrust of moderated regression can also be expressed in prediction terms, without reference to causality.

Overview of Book

In the remainder of this book, we discuss a wide range of issues regarding interaction effects. Our focus is primarily on the analysis of continuous independent variables, because excellent treatments already exist for the case of qualitative independent variables (e.g., Cohen and Cohen, 1983). In Chapter 2, we introduce traditional product term analysis as a means of analyzing bilinear interaction effects. We discuss methods for addressing questions about whether an interaction effect is present, the strength of the effect, and the nature of the effect. We also address the problems of levels of measurement and multicollinearity. In Chapter 3, we consider more advanced issues, including the formulation of standardized solutions in interaction analysis, power analysis, the problem of measurement error, incorporation of interaction effects into structural models, and the analysis of interactions between qualitative and continuous variables. In addition, we explore the strengths and weaknesses of alternative methods of interaction analysis that use "median split" strategies. In Chapter 4, we consider the analysis of interactions that are not bilinear in form. After a brief review of nonlinear relationships, we discuss methods for exploring interaction effects using polynomial regression and logarithms. A general method for specifying complex interactions in a multiple regression format is presented. Finally, we discuss methods for exploratory analysis of interaction effects. In Chapter 5, our attention turns to the analysis of moderated relationships in the context of correlation coefficients rather than slopes. We discuss methods for analyzing group differences between correlation coefficients where the moderator variable is either qualitative or quantitative in nature. In Chapter 6, we discuss substantive and practical issues in the analysis of interaction effects. This includes consideration of "false" interaction effects and reasons for failing to detect interaction effects when they are present. Finally, we provide a list of empirical applications of interaction analysis within a multiple regression context, and provide some concluding remarks on interaction analysis in general. Appendix B of the book provides computer programs that execute the major analyses discussed throughout all the chapters of this book.

2. TRADITIONAL PRODUCT TERM ANALYSIS

With Chapter 1 as background, we can proceed to the analysis of product terms and interaction effects in the context of multiple regression. In this chapter, we first identify three methods that have been used in the literature for analyzing moderated relationships. We focus our discussion on one of them, namely moderated multiple regression. We discuss basic issues for determining the presence of interaction effects, the strength of interaction effects, and the nature of interaction effects. We next discuss issues in the interpretation of regression coefficients and address two frequent criticisms of moderated multiple regression, the problem of levels of measurement and the problem of multicollinearity. Finally, we provide a numerical example that applies the concepts developed in the earlier portions of the chapter.

Consider the case of three continuous variables, where the investigator is interested in the effects of two independent variables (X_1 and X_2) on a dependent variable (Y). To use a concrete example, suppose that an investigator was interested in understanding why some teenagers engage in sex without using birth control, while other teenagers tend to use birth control. A sample of 125 sexually active female teenagers is studied, and for each teen a measure of their intention to use birth control is obtained. The measure consists of a rating scale with endpoints "definitely do not intend to use birth control" to "definitely intend to use birth control." Scores can range from 0 to 30, with higher scores indicating a stronger intention to use birth control. The researcher hypothesizes two general classes of factors that influence this intention. The first factor is the individual's personal feelings or attitude toward using birth control, that is, how favorable or unfavorable the individual personally feels about birth control. The second factor is the perceived peer pressure to use or not use birth control. Each of these factors, attitudes and perceived peer pressure, is measured on a five-point scale (see Ajzen and Fishbein, 1980, for a discussion of the types of scales that might be used in this type of research). For the attitude measure, the higher the score, the more favorable the individual personally feels about using birth control. For the peer pressure measure, low scores imply relatively little peer pressure to use or not use birth control. The higher the score, the more pressure the individual perceives from her friends.

As noted in Chapter 1, the test of an additive (or "main effects") model for predicting Y from X_1 and X_2 typically takes the form of a least squares regression equation such that

$$Y = a + b_1X_1 + b_2X_2 + e \qquad [2.1]$$

Execution of equation 2.1 involves regressing the measure of intention onto the measures of attitudes and peer pressure, respectively. Suppose that the investigator was interested in exploring the presence of an interaction effect. Specifically, the researcher hypothesizes that the relationship between attitudes and behavior is moderated by the amount of peer pressure that is present: When peer pressure is minimal, attitudes will exert a clear-cut effect on intentions. However, when peer pressure is strong, the influence of attitudes will be much less.

Three strategies are commonly used in the social science literature to test for such interaction effects. One strategy is to dichotomize X_1 and X_2 using median splits (or some other "cutting rule") and then to conduct a traditional 2 × 2 analysis of variance using Y as the dependent variable. A second strategy is to dichotomize the sample on the moderator variable (X_2), and then to compute the slopes for Y and X_1 for each of the two resulting groups. In our current example, the measure of peer pressure would be used to define two groups "low peer pressure" and "high peer pressure" by means of a median split. The slope of intentions on attitudes would then be computed for each of the two groups (using standard regression procedures), and these slopes would be formally compared statistically. The third strategy is to use multiple regression procedures. The regression strategy that is most popular is that recommended by Cohen and Cohen (1983). It involves forming a multiplicative term, X_1X_2, which is said to encompass the interaction effect, and to calculate two R^2 values, one for equation 2.1 and another for the following three-term equation:

$$Y = a + b_1X_1 + b_2X_2 + b_3X_1X_2 + e \qquad [2.2]$$

If an interaction effect is present, then the difference between the two R^2 values should be statistically significant (barring a Type I error). The formal significance test would use equation 1.3.

Suppose that the data in Table 2.1 were obtained for the example on birth control. These are hypothetical data and have been purposely constructed to illustrate later points in our discussion. For pedagogical purposes, the data can be arranged into a factorial table (via traditional analysis of variance), with mean Y scores represented at each combination of X_1 and X_2. This has been done in Table 2.2. In this table, we essentially have a 5 × 5 factorial design with equal n in each cell ($n = 5$).

Analyzing the data in Table 2.1 via standard multiple regression analysis without the product term yields a multiple R for the two-term additive model of 0.90139. The regression equation is

$$Y = 8 + 3X_1 + -2X_2 + e \qquad [2.3]$$

The multiple R for the three-term multiplicative model is 0.96825, and the regression equation is

$$Y = -1 + 6X_1 + 1X_2 + -1X_1X_2 + e \qquad [2.4]$$

Applying equation 1.3 yields the following:

$$F = \frac{(.96825^2 - .90139^2)/(3 - 2)}{(1 - .96825^2)/(125 - 3 - 1)}$$

$$= 242.26$$

For 1 and 121 degrees of freedom, the F is statistically significant, implying the presence of statistical interaction. This hierarchical F test yields the same substantive results as that of the t test for the statistical significance of b_3 in equation 2.2. For our data, the t for b_3 was 15.56. The square of this is the same as the observed F, namely (15.56)(15.56) = 242.26.

In the present chapter we consider basic issues in the analysis of moderated relationships using the product term approach. In Chapters 3 and 4, we consider more advanced issues in the execution of interaction analysis. We will also discuss the strengths and weaknesses of the alternative methods of interaction analysis in Chapter 3.

The Form of the Interaction

As noted, simple product terms permit the investigator to test for the presence of a moderated relationship. In principle, there is a wide variety of moderated relationships that can characterize an interaction effect between continuous variables. For example, one functional form is when the slope between Y and X_1 changes as a linear function of scores on X_2. This is called a *bilinear interaction*, and the data in Table 2.2 have this form. When peer pressure is low, equaling a score of 1, the slope of intentions on attitudes is high, namely 5: For every one unit that attitudes change, intentions are predicted to change five units. As peer pressure increases, the slope decreases. For example, when peer pressure equals 3, the slope of intentions on attitudes equals 3: For every one unit that attitudes change, intentions are predicted to change three units. Note that there is a straightforward linear relationship between changes in peer pressure and changes in the slope of intentions on attitudes. Every time peer pressure increases by one unit, the slope decreases by one unit. This orderly, monotonic, linear relationship between changes in the slope and changes in the moderator variable is the essence of statistical interaction, as measured by traditional product terms.

Other types of functional forms are possible. For example, it might be the case that changes in the intention-attitude slope are relatively large as one moves from low peer pressure to moderate amounts of peer pressure. However, as one progresses from moderate to high peer pressure the changes in slopes become less dramatic, until they reach a point of minimal change. Alternatively, the relationship between intentions and attitudes may be nonlinear in form. The *shape* (rather

TABLE 2.1
Raw Data for Numerical Example

Subject	Y	X_1	X_2	Subject	Y	X_1	X_2	Subject	Y	X_1	X_2
1	3	1	1	43	7	2	4	85	19	4	2
2	4	1	1	44	8	2	4	86	12	4	3
3	5	1	1	45	9	2	4	87	13	4	3
4	6	1	1	46	4	2	5	88	14	4	3
5	7	1	1	47	5	2	5	89	15	4	3
6	3	1	2	48	6	2	5	90	16	4	3
7	4	1	2	49	7	2	5	91	9	4	4
8	5	1	2	50	8	2	5	92	10	4	4
9	6	1	2	51	13	3	1	93	11	4	4
10	7	1	2	52	14	3	1	94	12	4	4
11	3	1	3	53	15	3	1	95	13	4	4
12	4	1	3	54	16	3	1	96	6	4	5
13	5	1	3	55	17	3	1	97	7	4	5
14	6	1	3	56	11	3	2	98	8	4	5
15	7	1	3	57	12	3	2	99	9	4	5
16	3	1	4	58	13	3	2	100	10	4	5
17	4	1	4	59	14	3	2	101	23	5	1
18	5	1	4	60	15	3	2	102	24	5	1
19	6	1	4	61	9	3	3	103	25	5	1
20	7	1	4	62	10	3	3	104	26	5	1
21	3	1	5	63	11	3	3	105	27	5	1
22	4	1	5	64	12	3	3	106	19	5	2
23	5	1	5	65	13	3	3	107	20	5	2
24	6	1	5	66	7	3	4	108	21	5	2
25	7	1	5	67	8	3	4	109	22	5	2
26	8	2	1	68	9	3	4	110	23	5	2
27	9	2	1	69	10	3	4	111	15	5	3
28	10	2	1	70	11	3	4	112	16	5	3
29	11	2	1	71	5	3	5	113	17	5	3
30	12	2	1	72	6	3	5	114	18	5	3
31	7	2	2	73	7	3	5	115	19	5	3
32	8	2	2	74	8	3	5	116	11	5	4
33	9	2	2	75	9	3	5	117	12	5	4
34	10	2	2	76	18	4	1	118	13	5	4
35	11	2	2	77	19	4	1	119	14	5	4
36	6	2	3	78	20	4	1	120	15	5	4
37	7	2	3	79	21	4	1	121	7	5	5
38	8	2	3	80	22	4	1	122	8	5	5
39	9	2	3	81	15	4	2	123	9	5	5
40	10	2	3	82	16	4	2	124	10	5	5
41	5	2	4	83	17	4	2	125	11	5	5
42	6	2	4	84	18	4	2				

than the slope) of the curve between the independent variable and dependent variable may change as a function of peer pressure; and so on.

The number of possible functional forms of moderated relationships between continuous variables is infinite. An important point to consider is that simple product terms, as used in equation 2.2, test for only one functional form, namely a bilinear interaction effect (within certain constraints). Failure to obtain a statistically significant interaction using traditional product terms may reflect the presence of an alternative functional form rather than the absence of a moderated relationship. The ideal situation is where a theory predicts the presence of a specific functional form, and an appropriate analytic strategy is derived in order to test the theory. The importance of theory in conducting interaction analysis cannot be emphasized strongly enough. Ultimately, theory will guide the specification of an interaction model. We will discuss this issue in more depth in later chapters. For the present, we restrict our attention to the analysis of bilinear interactions of the traditional form involving one dependent variable, one independent variable, and one moderator variable.

The Test for the Presence of an Interaction Effect

As noted earlier, there are three questions to be addressed in the analysis of interaction effects: (1) Is there an interaction effect in the population, based on the analysis of sample data; (2) if so, what is the strength of the effect; and (3) if so, what is the nature of the effect? We will discuss each of these questions, in turn.

The test for the presence of statistical interaction was described above: If the hierarchical F test for equation 2.2 versus equation 2.1 is statistically significant, then this is consistent with the presence of a (bilinear) moderated relationship. Technically, the null hypothesis that is being evaluated is that the regression coefficient for the product term is zero in the population. Rejection of this hypothesis is consistent with the notion that a bilinear interaction is present.

Although it is not always recognized as such, product terms, by and of themselves, do not necessarily represent statistical interactions. This is because a product term typically is correlated with its constituent parts. It therefore represents a complex amalgamation of variance due to "main effects" as well as to interactions. For this reason, it is necessary to partial the component parts of the product term from the term itself when evaluating the presence of a moderated relationship. This is the essence of the hierarchical test.

The Strength of the Effect

The strength of the interaction effect can be evaluated by means of an "eta-squared-like" statistic. Specifically, the difference between the squared multiple correlation for equation 2.2 and the squared multiple correlation for equation 2.1 reflects the strength of the interaction effect in the sample data. In the birth control example, the two-term additive model yielded a squared multiple correlation of 0.811, whereas the three-term "interaction" model yielded a squared multiple correlation of 0.937. The "strength" of the moderated relationship was

Table 2.2
Cell Means as a Function of X_1 and X_2

			X_2		
X_1	1	2	3	4	5
5	25	21	17	13	9
4	20	17	14	11	8
3	15	13	11	9	7
2	10	9	8	7	6
1	5	5	5	5	5

therefore $0.937 - 0.811 = 0.126$. The interaction effect accounts for 12.6% of the variance in intentions to use birth control.

The Nature of the Effect

Given a statistically significant interaction effect, it is of interest to specify the nature of the interaction. Since we are evaluating an interaction effect that has a bilinear functional form, the nature of the relationship can be discerned by examination of b_3 in the three-term equation. b_3 indicates the number of units that the slope of Y on X_1 changes, given a one-unit change in X_2. In our example, the value of b_3 is -1. This implies that for every one unit that peer pressure increases, the slope of intentions on attitudes decreases one unit. That this is indeed the case is readily apparent from inspection of Table 2.2.

The data in Table 2.2 are hypothetical, and the slope of Y on X_1 at a given value of X_2 is evident from visual inspection of the data. However, rarely will data be so orderly in practice. As it turns out, it is possible to calculate the effects of X_1 on Y for any given value of X_2 using the regression coefficients from the three-term regression equation. All that is required is some algebraic manipulation.

We begin by specifying a value of X_2 (peer pressure) where we want to analyze the relationship between Y and X_1. Let us begin with the lowest score possible on X_2, namely a value of 1. Using the three term equation, we substitute the score of 1 wherever X_2 occurs. This yields

$$Y = -1 + 6X_1 + (1)(1) + (-1)(X_1)(1) + e$$

We can rearrange the right side of the equation to group all of the terms with an X_1 to the right:

$$Y = -1 + (1)(1) + 6X_1 + (-1)(X_1)(1) + e$$

Then we can factor X_1 out of the relevant terms.

$$Y = -1 + (1)(1) + X_1[6 + (-1)(1)] + e$$

which, in turn, yields

$$Y = 0 + 5X_1 + e$$

This yields the linear equation describing the relationship between Y and X_1 when X_2 equals 1. Let us now perform the same calculations using the highest X_2 score of 5. Substituting a score of 5 for X_2 yields

$$Y = -1 + 6X_1 + (1)(5) + (-1)(X_1)(5) + e$$

Performing the same calculations produces the following result:

$$Y = 4 + 1X_1 + e$$

These calculations reveal how the relationship between Y and X_1 varies over the range of X_2 values: At low values of X_2 (i.e., 1) a one-unit increase in X_1 is associated with a five-unit predicted increase in Y. At high values of X_2 (i.e., 5), a one-unit increase in X_1 is associated with a one-unit predicted increase in Y.

We can formally state an equation for calculating the slope of the predicted effects of X_1 on Y at any particular value of X_2. It is

$$b_1 \text{ at } X_2 = b_1 + b_3 X_2 \qquad [2.5]$$

To illustrate from our example, the slope of Y on X_1 when X_2 equals 4 is

$$b_1 \text{ at } 4 = 6 + (-1)(4) = 2$$

With the above as background, we are in a position to consider more advanced issues in the analysis of simple product terms.

The Interpretation of Regression Coefficients

One such issue is the interpretation of the regression coefficients for X_1 and X_2. Several social scientists have argued that the inclusion of a multiplicative term yields regression coefficients that are difficult to interpret (e.g., Blalock, 1969; Wright, 1976). Allison (1977), Althauser (1971), and Smith and Sasaki (1979) all have suggested that a multiplicative term undermines the interpretability of the regression coefficients associated with X_1 and X_2. Some researchers have observed that these coefficients may reverse themselves in sign and relative magnitude when a product term is added to a traditional two-term equation. Such "contradictions" supposedly make difficult interpretation of the regression coefficients in the model with multiplicative terms.

In actuality, regression coefficients yielded in the three-term equation are subject to meaningful interpretation. Differences such as those noted above occur because the coefficients in the two equations (equation 2.1 versus 2.2) estimate different concepts. In the two-term "main effects only" model, a regression coefficient estimates the effects of the independent variable on the dependent variable, across the levels of the other independent variables: b_1 reflects the trends of change in Y with changes in X_1 at each level of X_2, and b_2 reflects the trends of change in Y with changes in X_2 at each level of X_1. In contrast, in the model with a multiplicative term, the regression coefficients for X_1 and X_2 reflect *conditional* relationships: b_1 reflects the influence of X_1 on Y when X_2 equals zero, and b_2 reflects the influence of X_2 on Y when X_1 equals zero. Differences in the values of b_1 and b_2 coefficients for the two different models result from the fact that in the "main effects" model, the coefficients estimate "general" relationships at each level of the other independent variable, whereas in the product-term model, they estimate conditional relationships, that is, the case where all X variables but the one in question equal zero.[2]

The distinction between regression coefficients in the two models holds with equal vigor for standard errors of those coefficients: The standard errors for regression coefficients in the additive model reflect estimates of sampling error across levels of the independent variables. In contrast, the standard errors for regression coefficients in the interactive model are conditional and reflect sampling error when the other variables equal a specific value, namely zero. Thus, the standard error for b_1 in equation 2.2 estimates sampling error for the regression coefficient when X_2 equals zero. Similarly, the standard error for b_2 in equation 2.2 estimates sampling error for the coefficient when X_1 equals zero.

In the previous section, we showed how one could calculate the slope of Y on X_1 for any given value of X_2 by using equation 2.5. It is also possible to calculate the standard error for this coefficient by means of the following equation:

$$s(b_1 \text{ at } X_2) = [(\text{var}(b_1) + X_2^2 \text{var}(b_3) + 2X_2 \text{cov}(b_1, b_3)]^{1/2} \qquad [2.6]$$

where $\text{var}(b_1)$ is the variance of the b_1 regression coefficient, $\text{var}(b_3)$ is the variance of the b_3 regression coefficient, and $\text{cov}(b_1, b_3)$ is the covariance of the b_1, b_3 regression coefficients. The variance and covariance terms on the right-hand side of the equation are readily obtained from standard computer output. For example, in SPSS-X, the option COVB within the REGRESSION program yields the variance and covariance of the coefficients, under the title "Var-Covar Matrix of Regression Coefficients (B)." Calculation of the standard error is useful for conducting the ANOVA analog of simple main effects analysis, as will now be demonstrated.

Simple Effects and "Interaction Comparison" Analysis of Regression Coefficients

Given a statistically significant interaction effect, most investigators will want to gain an intuitive feel for the interaction by calculating the slope of Y on X_1 at a few different values of X_2. The decision as to which values of the moderator variable to use should be theoretically guided. In the absence of theory, a reasonable strategy is to evaluate the effects of X_1 on Y at "low," "medium," and "high" values of X_2, where "low" might be defined as one standard deviation below the mean X_2 score, "medium" as the mean, and "high" as one standard deviation above the mean. Equations 2.5 and 2.6 can then be used to define the relevant coefficients and their associated standard errors.

Once the relevant coefficients and standard errors have been computed, it is possible to test the statistical significance of each coefficient. This procedure is directly analogous to simple main effects analysis in analysis of variance strategies. The test of the regression coefficient for b_1 at a given value of X_2 takes the form of a t test, such that

$$t = (b_1 \text{ at } X_2)/s(b_1 \text{ at } X_2) \qquad [2.7]$$

where X_2 is the value of X_2 at which the effects of X_1 on Y are to be tested. The value in equation 2.7 is approximately distributed as t with $N-k-1$ degrees of freedom, where k is the number of predictor terms in the interactive model (in this case, k = 3). A numerical example illustrating the use of equation 2.7 is presented in a later section.

The above strategy involves the computation of multiple t tests (one for each value of X_2 that is being evaluated), which introduces the problem of inflated Type I error rates across the multiple tests (i.e., inflated experimentwise error rates). This can be controlled, if appropriate, using a Bonferroni procedure. The procedure involves setting a per-comparison alpha level of 0.05 divided by the number of tests performed. Alternatively, if statistical power is a concern, an adjusted Bonferroni procedure can be used (see, for example, Holland and Copenhaver, 1988[3]).

In Chapter 1, we stated that researchers frequently use a technique called interaction comparisons to decompose an interaction effect. In regression terminology, interaction comparisons reveal slope differences as one moves from one value of the moderator variable to another. This information is readily available in b_3 (and its associated test of significance) and, hence, no tests corresponding to interaction comparisons are necessary. The nature of the interaction effect is bilinear in form, and, for every one unit that X_2 changes, the slope of Y on X_1 changes b_3 units.

Levels of Measurement

Several social scientists have argued that interactive regression analysis is applicable only when the measures of X_1 and X_2 are on ratio scales (e.g., Southwood, 1978). The idea is that regression coefficients are meaningless if trivial transformations in scaling affect substantive results. Cohen (1978) shows that simple additive transformations (e.g., adding a constant of 50) to a given X variable can change the regression coefficients, standard errors, and significance tests of the other X variables. Because interval scales have arbitrary zero points, additive transformations are trivial theoretically. The fact that such transformations affect the results of the regression analysis are therefore taken to imply that interval scales are inappropriate for models with multiplicative terms. This is not the case.

The impact of an additive transformation on an interactive model can be clarified by considering its conditional nature. Additive transformations of an X variable shift the zero point used to describe the conditional relationships. Consider our example with intentions to use birth control. Suppose we perform an additive transformation on the peer pressure scores (X_2) by subtracting the mean peer pressure value from each score (in this case, the mean is 3). Such a transformation is referred to as "centering." As it turns out, this transformation will leave unchanged the values of b_2 and b_3, but will alter the values (and standard errors) of b_1 and the intercept. The pre-transformation regression equation is

$$Y = -1 + 6X_1 + 1X_2 + -1X_1X_2 + e \qquad [2.8]$$

and the posttransformation regression equation is

$$Y = 2 + 3X_1 + 1X_2 + -1X_1X_2 + e \qquad [2.9]$$

The change in b_1 in the two equations (from 6 to 3) occurs because the conditional relationship of the influence of X_1 on Y is being evaluated at a different zero point than was originally the case. In the pretransformation analysis, the zero point was based on a scale that was three units higher than the posttransformation X_2 (peer pressure) score. When X_2 is centered, the zero point occurs at the mean. If in the original analysis we wanted to evaluate the impact of X_1 on Y at the mean of X_2, we could do so by substituting the mean value for X_2 in equation 2.8 and then, by algebraic manipulation (or the application of equation 2.5), calculate the slope of Y on X_1:

$$Y = -1 + 6X_1 + (1)(3) + (-1)X_1(3) + e$$

$$= 2 + 3X_1 + e$$

Note that the observed slope equals the slope for X_1 in the posttransformation equation where X_2 was centered. Centering (or any other additive transformation) has no effect on the substantive evaluation of the effect of X_1 on Y at a given value of X_2. It only changes the value of X_2 being evaluated (because with centering, a zero on X_2 corresponds to the mean, whereas without centering, this is not necessarily the case). In most cases, the choice of a value of X_2 at which to evaluate effects of X_1 on Y will be theoretically driven or will focus on the "high," "medium," and "low" scores defined earlier. Given this, it is entirely appropriate to evaluate interaction effects for interval level data.

Although the evaluation of product terms is appropriate for interval level data, use of the approach on ordinal level data (as though the data had interval characteristics) is controversial. Busemeyer and Jones (1983) present a convincing case for the biasing effects of departures from interval level data. Borgatta and Bohrnstedt (1980), on the other hand, argue that most social scientists have not been led astray by the assumption of intervality — or, more formally, linearity of responses (see Birnbaum, 1982). Strictly speaking, the regression approach with continuous variables assumes interval-level data. However, ordinal data may be analyzed if such data approximate interval-level characteristics. The core of the controversy is how close an approximation is needed for conclusions not to be suspect. A detailed consideration of this issue is well beyond the scope of this monograph. Interesting perspectives on the measurement level controversy are provided by Townsend and Ashby (1984) and Maxwell and Delaney (1984). Suffice it to say that the analysis of interaction effects between continuous variables with noninterval data is controversial.

Simple Transformations and Multicollinearity

A complaint against the use of multiplicative terms in regression analysis focuses on the issue of multicollinearity (e.g., Althauser, 1971; Blalock, 1979). Critics have noted that multiplicative terms usually exhibit strong correlations with the component parts (X_1 and X_2), introducing "inflated" standard errors for the regression coefficients. The adverse effects of multicollinearity for the general case of multiple regression are well-known and need not be reiterated here (e.g., Darlington, 1968; Gordon, 1986; Johnston, 1972). Because multiplicative terms can introduce high levels of multicollinearity, critics have recommended against their use.

The problem of multicollinearity in interaction analysis can be placed in perspective by keeping in mind the conditional nature of the interactive model. Specifically, it can be shown that the standard errors for the conditional coefficients in the interactive model will, for some value of X_1 and X_2, always be *lower* than the standard errors for the corresponding coefficients for X_1 and X_2 in the additive model, given the presence of statistical interaction (Kmenta, 1986). Of interest to the present discussion is the identification of values of X_2 at which the conditional standard error for the effects of X_1 on Y is minimal. This value can be found by differentiating equation 2.6 with respect to X_2, equating to zero, and then solving for X_2 (Friedrich, 1982). This yields

$$\min X_2 = -\text{cov}(b_1, b_3)/\text{var}(b_3) \qquad [2.10]$$

Returning to our birth control example, equation 2.10, with the help of an SPSS-X derived matrix of variances and covariances, can be used to identify the value of X_2 at which the minimum standard error of b_1 occurs. This value is

$$\min X_2 = -(-.01240)/.00413 = 3$$

Equation 2.6 can be used to calculate the standard error for this score:

$$s(b_1 \text{ at } 3) = [.04545 + 3^2(.00413) + 2(3)(-.01240)]^{1/2}$$

$$= 0.0909$$

The standard errors for b_1 across the range of X_2 values can be calculated by substituting the low score (1) and the high score (5) of X_2 into equation 2.6, which yields the values 0.1575 and 0.1575, respectively (in this example, the two standard errors are equal, but this will not always be the case). As scores on X_2 deviate from the minimizing score (3), the standard errors of the b_1 will increase. Thus, the standard errors of b_1 across the observed range of X_2 vary from 0.1575 when $X_2 = 1$, down to a minimum of 0.0909 when $X_2 = 3$, and up to a maximum of 0.1575 when $X_2 = 5$. It is interesting to note that the standard error for b_1 in the additive model (which equals 0.1568) occurs between the minimum (0.0909) and the maximum (0.1575) values. Again, the standard error in the additive model represents a "generalized" standard error across X_2 values.

As evident from the above discussion, the major threat of multicollinearity in interactive models is not substantive (see Cronbach, 1987) but rather practical. Multicollinearity does not affect the properties of OLS estimates (i.e., such estimates are BLUE unless there is complete multicollinearity). High correlations between predictors, however, can cause computational errors on standard computer programs, given the algorithms that are typically used for regression analysis. Cronbach (1987) suggests centering the X_1 and X_2 variables (prior to forming the multiplicative term) as a means of addressing this problem. Such a transformation will tend to yield low correlations between the product term and the component parts of the term. We also recommend the transformation suggested by Cronbach.

A Numerical Example

At this point, a concrete example will help to summarize our discussion. In a sociological study, 100 religious Catholics from a midwestern community were asked how many children they desired to have in their completed family (Y). In addition, they were asked to indicate the number of children there were in the family that they were raised in (X_1), as well as their current family income (X_2), measured in units of $1,000 (e.g., a score of 15 = $15,000). The means and standard deviations for the three measures are provided in Table 2.3. The X_1 and X_2 scores were centered (i.e., deviation scores were formed), and the product of the centered scores was computed for each subject. A multiple regression analysis was then conducted regressing Y onto X_1, X_2, and X_1X_2, using the SPSS-X multiple regression computer program (note: hereafter, X_1 and X_2 will refer to centered scores). Note that the correlations between the product term (X_1X_2) and its component (centered) parts are trivial in size ($r = -0.006$ and 0.019, respectively). This indicates that multicollinearity will not be a problem with respect to computational errors. The multiple correlation for the interaction model was 0.725 and the regression equation was

$$Y = 4.4279 + .81324X_1 + .0997X_2 + .0149X_1X_2 + e$$

The estimated standard errors for b_1, b_2, and b_3 were 0.098, 0.045, and 0.007, respectively.

We now evaluate our three basic questions concerning the presence, strength, and nature of the interaction effect. A t test of the b3 coefficient yields a statistically significant result ($t = 2.187$, p < 0.04). This suggests the presence of an interaction effect, as the t test yields the same conclusion as the hierarchical F test.

The strength of the effect is indexed by the difference in squared multiple correlations for the "main-effects only" model and the interactive model. For the former, the squared multiple correlation was 0.509, and for the later it was 0.526. This yields $0.526 - 0.509 = 0.017$. The interaction effect accounts for 1.7% of the variance in desired family size, a relatively small effect size.

To examine the nature of the interaction, we will use income (X_2) as the moderator variable. The value of b_3 indicates how the relationship between desired family size (DFS) and previous family size (PFS) varies across income.

For every $1,000 that income changes (which corresponds to "one unit" on X_2), the slope of DFS on PFS changes 0.0149 units. Let a "low" income score be defined as one standard deviation below the mean income and a "high" income score be defined as one standard deviation above the mean income. The standard deviation on income is 14.220. Because the data were centered, a low score corresponds to −14.220, the average score corresponds to 0, and a high score corresponds to +14.220. The slope of DFS on PFS when income is "average" (i.e., at the mean) can be obtained directly from the printout and corresponds to b_1. It equals 0.81324. Using equation 2.5, we can calculate the slopes for the case of a "low" income and a "high" income:

$$b_1 \text{ at } -14.220 = 0.81324 + (0.0149)(-14.220) = 0.603$$

$$b_1 \text{ at } +14.220 = 0.81324 + (0.0149)(+14.220) = 1.027$$

The standard error for b_1 when income is "average" is obtained directly from the printout and equals 0.09786. Using equation 2.6, we can calculate the standard errors for b_1 at "low" and "high" income values. This requires use of the variances and covariances of the regression coefficients, which are provided on the SPSS-X printout (as described earlier):

$$s(b_1 \text{ at } -14.22) = [.00958 + (-14.22^2)(.0000463761) \\ + 2(-14.22)(.0000131)]^{1/2} \\ = 0.136$$

$$s(b_1 \text{ at } +14.22) = [.00958 + (14.22^2)(.0000463761) \\ + 2(14.22)(.0000131)]^{1/2} \\ = 0.136.$$

The t ratios for the "low," "average," and "high" income values are computed by dividing the regression coefficients by their standard errors (e.g., t for −14.22 = 0.603/0.136 = 4.43).

The results of the above calculations can be summarized as follows:

Income Level	b_1	SE	t
Low	.603	.136	4.43
Average	.815	.098	8.33
High	1.027	.136	7.55

All of the t are statistically significant (using Bonferroni corrected alpha levels), indicating that all of the slopes differ from zero (barring a Type I error). At "low" levels of income, each additional child in one's past family translates into an additional 0.603 desired children in one's current family. At "average" levels of income, each additional child in one's past family translates into an additional 0.815 desired children in one's current family. At "high" levels of income, each additional child in one's past family translates into an additional 1.027 desired children in one's current family. For the present data, "low" income corresponds

Table 2.3

Means and Standard Deviations for Variables

Variable	Mean	SD
Desired Family Size	4.440	2.748
Past Family Size	2.960	1.601
Income	34.933	14.220

to \$20,713, the average income corresponds to \$34,933, and "high" income corresponds to \$49,153.

As noted earlier, the above t tests are analogous to simple main effects analysis in traditional ANOVA paradigms. Information pertinent to the regression analog of interaction comparisons is available from b_3: For every \$1,000 that income changes, the slope of desired family size on past family size increases by 0.0149 units.

3. ADDITIONAL ISSUES WITH
TRADITIONAL PRODUCT TERM ANALYSIS

Chapter 2 established basic principles of interactive regression analysis. In this chapter, we consider more advanced issues. First, we discuss the analysis of interaction effects in the context of standardized measures. We then discuss transformations for analyzing main effects and interaction effects simultaneously, when it is desirable to do so. The issue of statistical power and the minimization of Type II errors is addressed, as well as complications that are introduced by the presence of measurement error. We also discuss methods for incorporating moderated relationships into structural equation models. We then discuss complex interactions, namely those involving multiple moderated relationships and those involving a mixture of qualitative and continuous variables. Finally, we discuss the limitations of alternative methods that have been used in the social science literature for analyzing interactive relationships.

Standardized Solutions

As noted in Chapter 1, some investigators prefer to interpret standardized regression coefficients in the context of certain multiple regression applications. The traditional practice is to standardize both the dependent variable and all of the independent variables. This practice is problematic in the analysis of product terms. Although such transformations will not affect the significance test of the interaction, nor the estimates of its effect size, they will affect the interpretability of the regression coefficients. The key to interaction analysis is the ability to factor X_1 from the weighted product term $b_3X_1X_2$ and b_1X_1. To do so with standard scores, the terms in the equation need to equal $b_3Z_1Z_2$ and b_1Z_1, where Z_1 is the standard score on X_1, and Z_2 is the standard score on X_2. This is not the case in the standardized solution generated by computer programs. Rather, the product term represents the standardization of $X_1 X_2$ (or $Z_1 {}_2$), yielding $b_3 Z_1 {}_2$ and $b_1 Z_1$. This undermines the conditional interpretation of b_3.

If a "standardized" solution is desired, then one approach would be to standardize the Y, X_1 and X_2 scores prior to analysis, form the product of the Z_1 and Z_2 scores for each subject, and then use the standardized scores and the $Z_1 Z_2$ product term for purposes of analysis (Friedrich, 1982). Interpretation would then focus on the unstandardized regression coefficients as described above, but these would now reflect "standardized" coefficients (i.e., they can be interpreted in the spirit of standardized scores). Such an analysis may yield a nonzero intercept term, but this generally will be of little theoretical consequence. The b_1 will reflect the number of Z scores that Y is predicted to change given a one Z score increase in X_1 when $Z_2 = 0$, that is, when X_2 equals its mean value. The b_2 will reflect the number of Z scores that Y is predicted to change given a one Z score increase in X_2 when $Z_1 = 0$, that is, when X_1 equals its mean value. The b_3 indicates that for every one Z score that X_2 increases, the slope of Z_Y on Z_1 changes by b_3 units. In practice, the values of b_1 and b_2 in the "standardized" version of equation 2.1 will tend to approximate the values of the corresponding standardized regression coefficients in the "main effects only."

The Interpretation of Main Effects in the Presence of a Significant Interaction

As noted in Chapter 1, some researchers find it meaningful on occasion to interpret main effects in the presence of statistical interaction if the main effect is viewed in terms of an average effect. When the independent variable and moderator variables are centered, the unstandardized regression coefficient for the independent variable reflects its influence on the dependent variable at the average value of the moderator variable. This coefficient usually will equal (or be very close to) the value of the regression coefficient for the independent variable in a main-effects-only model. If desired, it is possible to define a constant for X_1 and X_2, which, when subtracted from the respective raw scores, will yield *exactly* the value of the b_1 and b_2 regression coefficients in the main-effects-only model, without compromising the analysis of the interaction effect vis-à-vis b_3. The resulting deviation scores will be uncorrelated with their product term, and hence the product term is a "pure" index of interaction (i.e., it is not confounded with the main effects). The values of the constants are defined as

$$\text{Constant for } X_1 = -\text{cov}(b_2, b_3)/\text{var}(b_3) \qquad [3.1]$$

$$\text{Constant for } X_2 = -\text{cov}(b_1, b_3)/\text{var}(b_3) \qquad [3.2]$$

The values for the right-hand sides of equations 3.1 and 3.2 are obtained using the COVB option in SPSS-X. Note tat the standard errors for the transformed b_1 and b_2 coefficients may be different (lower) than those for the main effects only model. For a discussion of issues in the interpretation of coefficients that are centered via equations 3.1 and 3.2, see Tate (1984). For most applications, centering using means will suffice.

Power Analysis for Interaction Terms

When planning an investigation to explore interaction effects between continuous variables, the researcher may wish to determine the sample size that is needed to achieve a desired level of statistical power. Power refers to the probability of correctly rejecting the null hypothesis (or the probability of not making a Type II error). Power is important because with low statistical power it is possible that a theoretically important interaction effect will go undetected by the researcher.

The significance test for an interaction effect takes the form of a hierarchical multiple regression analysis (vis-à-vis equation 1.3). Four factors must be specified to determine the necessary sample size for such tests. First, one must specify the desired level of power of the statistical test. This varies across substantive areas and will depend on the seriousness of a Type II error. In the absence of substantive guidelines, Cohen (1988) recommends that power of 0.80 be sought, although he recognizes that this criterion is arbitrary (see Cohen,1988, for an excellent discussion of the relevant issues). Second, one must specify the Type I error rate (alpha level) for the test. This is traditionally set at 0.05 in the social sciences, although the consequences of committing a Type I error should be considered when making this determination. Third, one must estimate what the population squared multiple correlation is for the main-effects-only model, and, fourth, one must estimate the population squared multiple correlation for the "full" model (that includes the product term). The difference between these two estimates is the estimated strength of the interaction effect. Often, it is difficult for an investigator to make these latter two estimations. Estimates can be based on previous research, theoretical guidelines, pilot research, and/or common sense. If the researcher lacks confidence in his or her estimates, then he or she can err toward conservatism (and an increased sample size) by assuming relatively small squared multiple correlations and interaction effects in the population.

The estimation of necessary sample sizes to achieve *a priori* levels of power is complex, and a complete treatment of this topic is well beyond the scope of this monograph. Interested readers are referred to Cohen (1988). However, to gain some appreciation for the issue, Table 3.1 presents approximate sample sizes necessary to achieve a power of 0.80 for alpha = 0.05 (two-tailed) in the case of one continuous independent variable and one continuous moderator variable. The rows represent different estimates of squared multiple correlations for the main-effects-only model, and the columns represent different estimates of squared multiple correlations for the full model. For example, if an investigator conjectured that the squared multiple correlation in the population for the main-effects-only model is 0.10 and that the corresponding squared multiple correlation for the full model is 0.20, then the approximate sample size that is needed to achieve power of 0.80 for testing the interaction effect at alpha = 0.05 is 65. As another example, if the investigator conjectured that the squared multiple correlation in the population for the main-effects-only model is 0.20 and that the corresponding squared multiple correlation for the full model is 0.25, then the approximate sample size to achieve power of 0.80 for testing the interaction effect at alpha = 0.05 is 119.

Several points should be made about the entries in Table 3.1. First, the smaller the population multiple R is in the two equations, the lower will be the statistical power (and the greater the sample size that will be needed). Second, although it is not evident in Table 3.1, the greater the number of interaction terms, the lower the power, everything else being equal. For example, for three interaction terms and squared multiple Rs of 0.01 and 0.03, the requisite sample size to achieve power of 0.80 would be 520 instead of the 380 entry in Table 3.1 (Cohen, 1988). Finally, the entries in Table 3.1. are only approximate and probably lower bound estimates, because, they assume normality in all predictors.

Structural Equation Models

Social scientists frequently use structural equations to test causal models (Asher, 1976). A common method for summarizing the parameter estimates within a causal model is that of the path diagram. In path diagrams, a causal influence from X to Y is represented by a straight arrow emanating from X and extending to Y (see Figure 1.1). A correlational (noncausal) relationship is represented by a curved arrow between the variables. Consider the model in Figure 3.1A. According to this model, the amount of salary that factory workers are paid is directly influenced by how long they have been employed by a company (measured in years) and by the quality of their work (as indexed by the number of products manufactured by the factory that they produce in a day). The quality of their work, in turn, is influenced by how long they have been employed by the company. There are no interaction effects in this model. To determine the values of the structural coefficients for arrows leading to a given variable, one regresses that variable onto all variables with an arrow extending directly to it. For example, to determine the values of paths b and c, one would regress salary (Y) onto quality (X_1) and the number of years employed (X_2), using multiple regression procedures. The regression coefficient for X_1 would be the least squares estimate of path b and the regression coefficient for X_2 would be the least squares estimate of path c. To determine the value of path a, one would regress quality of work onto the number of years employed. The resulting regression coefficient is the least squares estimate of the value of path a.

In contrast to this, the model in Figure 3.1B posits all of the same relationships, but includes an interaction effect. In this model, quality of work influences salary, but the effect is moderated by the number of years that a person has been employed with the company (e.g., the more seniority, the less the impact that quality of work has on salary). To estimate the values of the paths b,c, and d in this model, X_1 (quality) and X_2 (number of years on the job) are first centered, and a product term ($X_1 X_2$) is then computed. Salary is regressed onto all three terms using multiple regression. The regression coefficient for X_1 is the value of b, the

TABLE 3.1

Approximate Sample Sizes Necessary for Achieving Power of 0.80 for
Alpha = 0.05 With One Interaction Term

R_1^2	R_2^2											
	0.01	0.03	0.05	0.10	0.15	0.20	0.25	0.30	0.35	0.40	0.45	0.50
0.01		380	188	90	49	35	27	21	17	14	12	10
0.03			372	102	58	39	29	22	18	15	13	10
0.05				143	68	43	32	24	19	15	13	10
0.10					135	65	41	29	22	17	14	12
0.15						127	60	39	27	21	16	13
0.20							119	57	36	25	19	15
0.25								111	53	33	24	17
0.30									103	49	31	22
0.35										95	45	28
0.40											88	41
0.45												80

R_1 = 2 predictors; $Y = a + b_1X_1 + b_2X_2 + e$
R_2 = 3 predictors; $Y = a + b_1X_1 + b_2X_2 + b_3X_1X_2 + e$

regression coefficient for X_2 is the value of c, and the regression coefficient for X_1X_2 is the value of d. In this case, c represents the effects of number of years on the job on salary when quality of work is average (i.e., at its mean value). Similarly, b represents the effects of quality of work on salary when the number of years on the job is average. The value of d indicates how much the effects of quality of work on salary changes, given a one-year change in experience. The value for the path of a is determined using the same procedures as in Figure 3.1A.

The parameter estimates of a model that includes an interaction effect can be summarized in a path diagram by substituting the values of the estimates for the letters in Figure 3.1B. Alternatively, one might omit the d path altogether, and present three versions of the model containing values of $a,b,$ and c. In one version, the values of $a,b,$ and c would reflect the parameter estimates when the moderator variable (X_2) is high (e.g., one standard deviation above the mean); in the second version, the values of $a,b,$ and c would reflect the parameter estimates when the moderator variable is average (i.e., at its mean); and in the third version, the values of $a,b,$ and c would reflect the parameter estimates when the moderator variable is low (e.g., one standard deviation below the mean). This latter form of presentation may be prohibitive if there is more than one moderated relationship in the model. Of course, additional statistics surrounding model evaluation (e.g., indices of model fit, residual variances, simple effects analysis, and so on) would also be reported. Decomposition of effects with interactive structural equation models (in terms of direct effects, indirect effects, spurious effects, and unanalyzed relationships) follows standard decompositional procedures (see Pedhazur, 1982). For another approach to the presentation of interaction effects in path diagrams, see Hayduk and Wonnacutt (1980).

The Problem of Measurement Error

It is well known that unreliable measures can yield biased estimates of regression coefficients in multiple regression or structural equation analysis (e.g., Bohrnstedt and Carter, 1971). Social scientists frequently conduct research using fallible measures. Measurement error is thus a potential problem for the analysis of interaction effects involving continuous variables.

Using classical test theory, Busemeyer and Jones (1983) show that measurement error has the effect of attenuating hierarchical evaluations of product terms. The degree of attenuation is a direct function of the reliability of the product term, which we will call Pr. Under standard statistical assumptions, the amount of attenuation in changes in R^2 will equal $Pr(R_2^2 - R_1^2)$. For example, if the true incremental explained variance $(R_2^2 - R_1^2)$ due to the addition of a product term is 0.20 and the reliability of the product term is 0.70, then the observed incremental explained variance will equal $(0.20)(0.70) = 0.14$, everything else being equal.

Under certain statistical constraints,[4] if the true correlation between X_1 and X_2 is zero, then the reliability of the product term $X_1 X_2$ will equal the reliability of X_1 times the reliability of X_2. Thus, if one measure is relatively reliable ($rX_1X_1 = 0.80$) and the second measure is relatively unreliable ($rX_2X_2 = 0.50$), then the reliability of the product will be lower than the reliability of the least reliable measure $[(0.80)(0.50) = 0.40]$. As the true correlation between X_1 and X_2 increases, the reliability of the product term will increase slightly, given the range of correlations and reliabilities typically observed in social science research (see Busemeyer and Jones, 1983, for elaboration). These facts underscore the difficulties that measurement error can create for hierarchical tests of interaction, especially in situations with low statistical power. Dunlap and Kemery (1987) evaluate the effects of unreliability on Type II errors for interaction analysis in a wide variety of situations involving a small sample size ($N = 30$). They observe reasonable levels of statistical power as long as the reliability of the constituent variables were both 0.80 or greater. However, it must be emphasized that even in these situations, complications result because of the fact that the least squares estimates of the regression coefficients are biased and inconsistent estimators. This, in turn, creates difficulties for the decomposition of a statistically significant interaction, depending on the nature and severity of the bias. Using large sample sizes can offset the loss of power induced by measurement error for purposes of hypothesis testing, but a large N will *not* necessarily eliminate complications due to bias in the regression coefficients (e.g., Busemeyer and Jones, 1983; Evans, 1985).

Several resolutions to the problem of measurement error have been proposed, none of which is entirely satisfactory. Cohen and Cohen (1975), Bohrnstedt and Marwell (1978), Heise (1986) and Fuller and Hidiroglu (1978) suggest approaches that require *a priori* knowledge of the reliabilities of the constituent variables. Cohen and Cohen (1983: 410) find fault with the method of correction that they suggested in their 1977 book, in that the approach tends to overestimate the size of the regression coefficients. The Bohrnstedt and Marwell approach has several limitations detailed by Busemeyer and Jones (1983). Heise (1986) finds

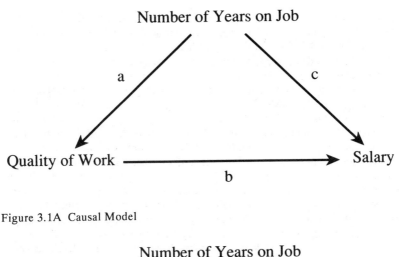

Figure 3.1A Causal Model

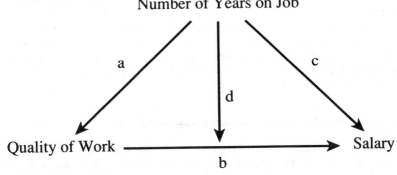

Figure 3.1B Causal Model

that his approach performed satisfactorily only under conditions where reliability was relatively high to begin with (e.g., above 0.90). The Fuller and Hidiroglu approach is promising, but has been developed only for models without multiplicative terms. Extensions of this approach to product term analysis would be valuable.

A second set of approaches to the problem of measurement error have used latent structural equation models. These approaches rely on multiple indicators of each construct to incorporate error theories into model tests and parameter estimation. Kenny and Judd (1984) point out the difficulties of applying traditional maximum likelihood approaches (e.g., **LISREL**) to product term analysis, and suggest an alternative approach based on a generalized least squares loss function (McDonald, 1978, 1985). A Monte Carlo simulation indicated that this approach was relatively successful at estimating the relevant population parameters under conditions of large sample size (N = 500). Unfortunately, the generalized loss function does not yield standard errors for the estimated coefficients, thereby limiting the utility of this approach. Jöreskog and Sörbom (1988) suggest modifications to **LISREL** which may be helpful in this regard (see also Hayduk, 1987: 232). Marsden (1983) presents an approach, based on block and instrumental variables, that also shows promise. When regression equations are to be compared among a small number of groups (e.g., where the moderator variable is gender), then the **LISREL** strategy can be used to good effect to take into account the biasing effects of measurement error (see Arvey, Maxwell, and Abraham, 1985, and the discussion in Chapter 4 on multigroup comparisions).

Statisticians are just beginning to address the problem of measurement error in interactive models, and we are optimistic about what the future holds. However, for the present, the biasing effects of measurement error must be acknowledged when empirically evaluating theoretical frameworks. Ignoring measurement error is tantamount to assuming perfect reliability. Probably the best method for counteracting the negative effects of unreliability in structural equation and multiple regression analysis is simply to use measures that have high reliability. This means that social scientists should devote considerable time and effort to developing high quality measures before embarking on complex theory tests. The literature in psychometrics, questionnaire construction, and psychophysics is replete with well-established recommendations for reducing measurement error and developing interval-level measurement techniques (e.g., providing judgement anchors, eliminating warm-effects). For useful discussions of these practices, see Anderson (1981), and Wegenar (1982).

Interaction with Three Continuous Independent Variables

Thus far, we have only considered the case where the moderated relationship involved three continuous variables: a dependent variable, an independent variable, and a moderator variable. The procedures are readily extended to cases involving four or more continuous variables. For example, consider the case of a single dependent variable, Y, and three X variables. The main-effects-only model is

$$Y = a + b_1 X_1 + b_2 X_2 + b_3 X_3 + e$$

A model for evaluating all two-way interactions is

$$Y = a + b_1 X_1 + b_2 X_2 + b_3 X_3 + b_4 X_1 X_2 + b_5 X_1 X_3 + b_6 X_2 X_3 + \text{e}.$$

A model evaluating the three-way interaction is

$$Y = a + b_1 X_1 + b_2 X_2 + b_3 X_3 + b_4 X_1 X_2 + b_5 X_1 X_3 + b_6 X_2 X_3$$

$$+ b_7 X_1 X_2 X_3 + e$$

Interpretation and evaluation of a two-way interaction has already been discussed in depth. With multiple two-way interactions, a regression coefficient associated with a given product term reflects the impact of the interaction effect, holding all other interactions and main effects constant. One issue that arises in multi-two-way equations concerns what to do with terms that yield negligible contributions (i.e., nonsignificant regression coefficients and zero correlations with the dependent variable). Some researchers drop nonsignificant terms and then reestimate the equation. Other researchers retain all of the terms irrespective of their statistical significance and interpret regression coefficients accordingly. The advantage to dropping terms with negligible impact is that it increases the degrees of freedom of the residual term, thereby increasing the power of the statistical test, everything else being equal. In addition, in certain instances, dropping negligible effects can have a positive influence on the standard errors of regression coefficients. The disadvantage to dropping terms with negligible impact is that their nonsignificance may be due primarily to low power, and the failure to be statistically significant may reflect a Type II error. Overall et al. (1981) show that, under such circumstances, deleting negligible terms can produce bias in the estimated regression coefficients. Our recommendation is as follows: If a given effect is predicted by a strong theory, but it fails to manifest itself in the data via a statistically significant regression coefficient, then it is probably best to include the relevant term in the overall equation. Although there may be a slight loss in statistical power, the gain in the quality of the coefficient estimates usually will be worthwhile. The inclusion or exclusion of a variable is first and foremost a theory problem and requires a theory-based solution. The issue should be dealt with first at the theoretical level and then only secondarily for statistical reasons (e.g., power or standard error concerns).

For the three-way model, the significance of the three-term interaction is again evaluated by means of the hierarchical test in equation 1.3 (testing the incremental R^2 of the full three-way model against the full two-way model). The strength of the three-way interaction effect is indexed by the difference in the squared multiple correlations for the full three-way model and the full two-way model. The nature of the interaction is reflected in b_7, which is interpreted as the number of units that Y changes per unit change in X_1 per unit change in X_2 per unit change in X_3. This takes on more clarity when expressed in terms of conditional effects: First, designate two variables (X_2 and X_3) as moderator variables and one variable (X_1) as the primary independent variable. For any given combination of values of X_2 and X_3, the intercept and slope of Y on X_1 can be specified. Using simple algebraic manipulation similar to that described in Chapter 2, the intercept is calculated from the following equation:

$$a \text{ at } (X_2, X_3) = a + b_2 X_2 + b_3 X_3 + b_6 X_2 X_3 \qquad [3.3]$$

and the slope is calculated from

$$b \text{ at } (X_2, X_3) = b_1 + b_4 X_2 + b_5 X_3 + b_7 X_2 X_3 \qquad [3.4]$$

As an example, suppose that the following regression equation was observed for the full three-way model:

$$Y = 2.0 + 1.0\,X_1 + 3.0\,X_2 + 2.5\,X_3 + 1.5\,X_1X_2 + 0.5\,X_1X_3$$

$$+ 3.5\,X_2X_3 + 4.0\,X_1X_2X_3 + e.$$

For the values of the moderator variables $X_2 = 5$ and $X_3 = 10$, the intercept is

$$a \text{ at } (5, 10) = 2.0 + (3.0)(5) + (2.5)(10) + (3.5)(5)(10) = 217.0$$

and the slope is

$$b \text{ at } (5, 10) = 1.0 + (1.5)(5) + (0.5)(10) + (4.0)(5)(10) = 213.5$$

it follows that the regression equation at this particular combination of X_2 and X_3 is

$$Y = 217.0 + 213.5X_1 + e.$$

Equations for any combination of the moderator variable values can thus be derived, and all principles discussed earlier readily apply. Calculation of the relevant conditional standard errors can be accomplished using the variance-covariance matrix of the regression coefficients and the appropriate expansion of equation 2.6 (see Appendix A).

The Case of a Qualitative Moderator and a Continuous Independent Variable

In some cases, an investigator may wish to evaluate an interaction effect when one of the predictors is a qualitative variable and the other is a continuous variable. This also is accomplished using the product-term approach. Consider the case where a psychologist is studying factors that influence high blood pressure. One variable that she thinks affects blood pressure is the stress that the individual experiences in his or her job: Individuals with higher stress occupations will be more likely to experience high blood pressure than individuals with lower stress occupations. The psychologist develops two treatment programs that she believes will reduce the impact of job stress on blood pressure. One of these programs is administered "in clinic" and involves multiple sessions with a psychologist. The second program consists of a series of exercises contained in an at-home manual. The psychologist devises an experiment in which 100 individuals participate in the at-home treatment, 100 individuals participate in the in-clinic treatment, and 100 individuals serve in a no-treatment control condition. The psychologist believes that the type of treatment (in-clinic" vs. at-home vs. control) will moderate the relationship between job stress and high blood pressure: The impact of job stress on blood pressure will be less for the treatment groups as opposed to the control group.

After participating in the relevant treatments, measures on an index of perceived job stress and an index of systolic blood pressure were obtained. The stress measure ranged from 0 to 30, with higher scores indicating greater amounts of perceived job stress. Blood pressure scores ranged from 110 to 160.

To execute the analysis, a set of "dummy" variables are defined for the qualitative variable. These dummy variables define group membership and permit an analysis of the effects of the qualitative variable on the dependent variable. A dummy variable is one in which the investigator assigns each individual in the experiment a score, based on his or her group membership. If the qualitative variable has k levels, then k-1 dummy variables are defined. In the present case, there are $3 - 1 = 2$ dummy variables. Any of three types of scoring procedures may be used for defining the scores on a dummy variable: (a) effect coding, (b) dummy coding, or (c) contrast coding (see Cohen and Cohen, 1983, for a discussion of the three approaches). We will use dummy coding to illustrate the analytic procedures. For the first dummy variable, members of one group (e.g., the in-clinic individuals) are all assigned scores of 1, and members of all other groups are assigned scores of 0. For the second dummy variable, members of another group (e.g., the in-home individuals) are all assigned scores of 1, and members of all other groups are assigned scores of 0. The group that is assigned zeros across all dummy variables is called the *reference group*. In this example, the reference group is the control group. The choice of the reference group is arbitrary. Table 3.2 illustrates the coding scheme.

The two dummy variables carry all the necessary information for defining group membership (see Cohen and Cohen, 1983, for a discussion of why $k-1$ dummy variables accomplish this). Next, the interaction between the qualitative and continuous independent variables is represented by creating $k-1$ additional dummy variables consisting of product terms. Specifically, the score on the continuous variable is multiplied by each dummy variable representing the qualitative variable. This operation also is illustrated in Table 3.2. Traditionally, dummy variables are *not* centered (see Chapter 2) for interpretational reasons that will be elaborated below. In this example, we also did not center the continuous independent variable, although such a transformation would be entirely appropriate if high levels of multicollinearity are expected.

The test of the significance of the interaction effect is accomplished by means of hierarchical regression using equation 1.3. First, a main-effects-only model is calculated by regressing blood pressure onto the measure of stress (S) and the two dummy variables (D_1 and D_2) representing the treatment condition. Second, a full-model multiple regression is conducted, regressing blood pressure onto all variables in Table 3.2, including the product terms, that is, the stress measure and D_1, D_2, D_1S and D_2S. The multiple correlation in the first case was 0.559, and in the second case, it was 0.606. The resulting regression equations are

$$BP = 143.265 + .563S + -23.525\,D_1 + -19.895\,D_2 + e$$

and

$$BP = 127.048 + 1.613S + 1.124D_1 + 2.493\,D_2 + -1.530\,D_1S$$

$$+ -1.461D_2S + e$$

In the first equation, the estimated standard errors for b_1, b_2 and b_3 were 0.142, 2.275, and 2.255, respectively. In the second equation, the estimated standard errors for b_1 through b_5 were 0.251, 6.165, 5.528, 0.349, and 0.333, respectively.

The test of the significance of the interaction effect is the hierarchical test of the main-effects-only model versus the full model. The resulting F is

$$F = \frac{(.606^2 - .559^2)/(5-3)}{(1 - .606^2)/(300 - 5 - 1)}$$

$$= 12.74$$

This F, with 2 and 294 degrees of freedom, is statistically significant. We can conclude that an interaction is present.

The strength of the interaction effect is $0.606^2 - 0.559^2 = 0.055$. The interaction effect accounts for 5.5% of the variance in blood pressure.

To discern the nature of the interaction effect, we need to calculate the slope of blood pressure on stress for each of the three groups. This is accomplished by use of the regression equation for the full model. Table 3.3 presents an abbreviated computer printout from an SPSS-X REGRESSION run using the full model. We will refer to this printout in the ensuing discussion. To determine the slope and intercept for the in-clinic group, we substitute the dummy codes that were assigned to that group wherever the relevant dummy variable occurs in the equation. For example, for this group, D_1 had a dummy code of 1, and D_2 had a dummy code of 0. This yields

$$BP = 127.048 + 1.613S + (1.124)(1) + (2.493)(0) + (-1.530)(1)S$$

$$+ -1.461(0)S + e$$

Using algebraic manipulation, we eliminate all terms that equal zero and collect all terms that have an S in them on the far right side of the equation:

$$BP = 127.048 + (1.124)(1) + 1.613S + (-1.530)(1)S + e$$

Next, we factor out the S variable from the terms on the right:

$$BP = 127.048 + 1.124 + S(1.613 - 1.530) + e$$

Finally, we total up the various scores, yielding the regression equation for group 1:

$$BP = 128.172 + 0.083S + e$$

For the in-clinic treatment group, the effect of stress on blood pressure corresponds to a slope of 0.083. For every one unit that stress increases, blood pressure is predicted to change 0.083 units.

We undertake the same calculations for the remaining groups. For the in-home group, the relevant dummy codes are $D_1 = 0$ and $D_2 = 1$. These values are substituted into the full-model equation wherever D_1 and D_2 occur, and the algebraic manipulations noted above are performed. This yields the following regression equation:

TABLE 3.2

Example of Effect Coding And Interaction Coding for a
Qualitative and Continuous Predictor

Individual	Group	Blood Pressure	Stress (S)	(Treatment)		(Interaction)	
				D_1	D_2	D_1S	D_2S
1	In-clinic	120	15	1	0	15	0
2	In-clinic	124	13	1	0	13	0
3	In-clinic	111	20	1	0	20	0
4	In-clinic	132	28	1	0	28	0
.	.	.	.	.	.	.	.
.	.	.	.	.	.	.	.
.	.	.	.	.	.	.	.
100	In-clinic	112	23	1	0	23	0
101	In-home	131	22	0	1	0	22
102	In-home	115	19	0	1	0	19
103	In-home	128	22	0	1	0	22
104	In-home	136	18	0	1	0	18
.	.	.	.	.	.	.	.
.	.	.	.	.	.	.	.
.	.	.	.	.	.	.	.
200	In-home	127	15	0	1	0	15
201	Control	111	20	0	0	0	0
202	Control	122	17	0	0	0	0
203	Control	119	22	0	0	0	0
204	Control	115	24	0	0	0	0
.	.	.	.	.	.	.	.
.	.	.	.	.	.	.	.
.	.	.	.	.	.	.	.
300	Control	118	24	0	0	0	0

$$BP = 129.541 + .152S + e$$

Finally, the dummy codes for the control group are $D_1 = 0$ and $D_2 = 0$. Substituting these values yields the following regression equation:

$$BP = 127.048 + 1.613S + e$$

It can be seen that the slopes for the two treatment groups are similar to each other, and both are quite distinct from that of the control group. A formal significance test of pairwise group differences can be derived from the significance tests for the regression coefficients associated with the product terms. b_4 is the unstandardized coefficient for D_1S, and b_5 is the unstandardized regression coefficient for D_2S. Notice that the value of b_4 equals the difference between the slope of the in-clinic group and the slope of the control group ($.083 - 1.613 = -1.530$). As it turns out, with dummy coding, the unstandardized regression coefficient for the product term will always equal the slope differences between the group coded 1 on the relevant dummy variable and the reference group. Thus, the value of b_5 equals (within rounding error) the difference between the slope of the in-home group and the slope of the control group $(0.152 - 1.613 = -1.461)$. The significance tests for b_4 and b_5 represent tests of the difference between slopes for the respective pair of groups. In our example, b_4 was statistically significant $(t = 4.38, p < 0.01)$, as was b_5 $(t = 4.39, p < 0.01)$, indicating that the slopes of both experimental groups differed from that of the control group. These pairwise tests are analogous to interaction comparisons in traditional ANOVA. It is also possible to test the differences in slopes for the two experimental groups, using information from the computer printout. However, some intermediate calculations are required.

First, one must compute the estimated standard error of the slope for each group separately. This is accomplished with reference to the variance-covariance matrix of the regression coefficients (see Table 3.3). Let D represent the dummy variable on which the group in question has a score of 1, let S represent the continuous independent variable (in this case, stress), let b_c represent the unstandardized regression coefficient for the continuous variable, and let b_p represent the unstandardized regression coefficient for the product term DS. Then the estimated standard error for group "g" is defined as

$$s(b \text{ for group } g) = [(\text{var}(b_c) + \text{var}(b_p) + 2\text{cov}(b_c, b_p)]^{1/2} \qquad [3.5]$$

For group 1, the standard error is

$$s(b \text{ for group } 1) = [.06298 + .12211 + 2(-.06298)]^{1/2}$$

$$= .243167$$

For group 2, the standard error is

$$s(b \text{ for group } 2) = [.06298 + .11087 + 2(-.06298)]^{1/2}$$

$$= .218838$$

The test for the difference in the slopes between groups 1 and 2 is:

$$t = \frac{(b \text{ for group } 1) - (b \text{ for group } 2)}{[s(b \text{ for group } 1)^2 + s(b \text{ for group } 2)^2]^{1/2}} \qquad [3.6]$$

In our example,

$$t = \frac{.083 - .152}{[.243167^2 + .218838^2]^{1/2}} = \frac{-.069}{.327} = -.211$$

The t is distributed with $N-k-1$ degrees of freedom, where k is the number of predictor variables in the full-term regression equation. For the present data, the t test of the differences in slopes between groups 1 and 2 is statistically nonsignificant.

The regression analog of simple main effects analysis requires a test of statistical significance of the observed slope for each group. That is, do the slopes 0.083 (in-clinic), 0.152 (in-home), and 1.613 (control), respectively, differ from

TABLE 3.3

Abbreviated SPSS Printout for Qualitative IV Example:
Interactive Model

			df	Sum of Squares		Mean Square		
Multiple R	.606	Regression	5	40,152.09		8,030.42		
R^2	.367	Residual	294	69,333.46		235.83		
		$F = 34.052$		Signif $F = 0.000$				

Variable	b	SE b	Beta	SE Beta	Correl	Part Cor	T	Sig T
D_1	1.124	6.165	.028	.152	−.303	.008	0.18	.855
D_2	2.492	5.528	.062	.136	−.221	.021	.45	.652
S	1.613	.251	.557	.087	.149	.298	6.43	.000
D_1S	−1.530	.349	−.725	.166	−.270	−.203	−4.38	.000
D_2S	−1.461	.333	−.624	.142	−.176	−.204	−4.39	.000
(Constant)	127.048	4.168					30.48	.000

Var-Covar Matrix of Regression Coefficients (b)

	D_1	D_2	S	D_1S	D_2S
D_1	38.00422				
D_2	17.37172	30.56396			
S	0.97237	0.97237	0.06298		
D_1S	−2.01186	−0.97237	−0.06298	0.12211	
D_2S	−0.97237	−1.69272	−0.06298	0.06298	0.11087

a hypothesized value of zero. This test is accomplished by dividing the slope for a given group by its standard error:

$$t = \frac{b \text{ for group } g}{s(b \text{ for group } g)} \qquad [3.7]$$

Equation 3.5 was used to calculate the relevant standard errors for all groups except the reference group. The standard error for the reference group is obtained directly from the computer printout, as it equals the standard error for the unstandardized regression coefficient for S. Thus, the tests of the slopes for groups 1, 2, and 3, respectively, are

$$t_1 = \frac{.083}{.243167} = .341$$

$$t_2 = \frac{.152}{.218838} = .695$$

$$t_3 = \frac{1.613}{.250958} = 6.427$$

The t is distributed with $N-k-1$ degrees of freedom. Only the slope for group 3, the control group, is significantly different from zero.

Alternative Approaches to Product-Term Analysis

Earlier, we mentioned two alternative approaches that have been used to analyze interaction effects between continuous variables. In this section, we briefly consider the utility of these approaches relative to the use of product terms in multiple regression.

2 × 2 Median Split Analysis. This strategy involves dichotomizing X_1 and X_2 using median splits (or some other "cutting rule") and then conducting a traditional 2 × 2 analysis of variance using Y as the dependent variable. A statistically significant interaction effect would indicate the presence of a moderated relationship. In general, this approach to the analysis of interaction effects is limited. As Cohen and Cohen (1983:309) cogently note, dichotomizing a continuous variable discards valuable information. It essentially reduces a multipoint scale to a two-point scale. Social scientists often go to great lengths to develop useful measures of personality, attitudes, intelligence, and other constructs that discriminate individuals on a continuum. These scales do not make two simple discriminations, "high" and "low." Rather, they discriminate a broad range of individuals. The researcher who dichotomizes a scale obliterates this precision, reducing the measure to two, somewhat crude, categories. This is not satisfactory.

On a statistical level, such dichotomization usually has adverse effects on both the percentage of variance that the dichotomized variable can account for and the statistical power. For example, if one assumes a normal distribution for a median-dichotomized variable, its squared correlation with the dependent variable (also assumed to be normally distributed) will be approximately 65% as large as the correlation between the graduated variables (Cohen and Cohen, 1983). Similar consequences occur for product terms, and, hence, the median split method can be problematic.

Although researchers should view scale reduction with caution, there are cases where it may be theoretically appropriate to induce reduction. As an example, suppose a developmental psychologist noted four types of thinking styles and hypothesized that these styles are age specific: children between the ages of 3 and 5 should exhibit style 1, children between the ages of 6 and 8 should exhibit style 2, children between the ages of 9 and 11 should exhibit style 3, and children between the ages of 12 and 14 should exhibit style 4. Suppose also that the styles are such that they could be ordered on a dimension of complexity; hence, they represent a quantitative variable. Assume that the hypothesis of the investigator is correct and that the relationship between style of thinking and membership in a given age group is perfect. In an analysis of a sample of 80 children, age can be scored and analyzed either continuously (using scores of 3, 4, 5, 6, 7, 8, 9, 10, and 11), or it can be grouped according to the a priori age categories and scored from 1 to 4. A correlation analysis between the variables would yield a lower correlation in the former case than in the latter case. In this instance, reduction of the age variable is theoretically meaningful (although one could argue that a better approach is to analyze the fully continuous data with nonlinear methods). Such instances are relatively rare in the social sciences.

Moderator Median Split Analysis. A second strategy for analyzing interaction effects is to dichotomize the sample on the moderator variable (X_2), and then to compute the slopes for Y on X_1 for each of the two resulting groups. The difference between the slopes is subjected to a test of statistical significance using the following equation:

$$t = \frac{b_j - b_k}{\{(SSE_j + SSE_k)/[(n_j + n_k) - 4)](\Sigma X_{1j} + \Sigma X_{1k})/(\Sigma X_{1j} \Sigma X_{1k})\}^{1/2}} \quad [3.8]$$

where b_j is the unstandardized regression coefficient for group j, b_k is the unstandardized regression coefficient for group k, SSE_j is the sum of squares error for group j, SSE_k is the sum of squares error for group k, n_j is the number of individuals in group j, n_k is the number of individuals in group k, ΣX_{1j} is the sum of the *squared* X_1 scores in group j, and ΣX_{1j} is the sum of the squared X_1 scores in group k. The t statistic in equation 2.1 is distributed with $n_j + n_k - 4$ degrees of freedom. A variant of this approach is to trichotomize the moderator variable and to conduct all pairwise comparisons of the slopes for the three groups.

This approach suffers the same limitations as the 2 × 2 median split approach. First, it reduces a more precise measure of the moderator variable to a two- (or three-) point index. Second, the approach yields tests of significance that are statistically less powerful than the product term approach. Thus, one is more likely to make a Type II error if the moderated relationship is truly bilinear in form. Finally, there is no intuitively interpretable index of the strength of the interaction effect (other than the size of the *t* ratio in equation 3.8). In contrast, the product term approach yields an index that is readily interpreted in terms of percent of variance accounted for.

Situations can occur where this form of analysis is more sensitive to the presence of interaction effects as compared to the traditional product term. For example, if an investigator trichotomizes the moderator variable and compares slopes for the three groups, he/she may observe statistically significant differences. In contrast, a product term approach applied to the same data may yield a statistically nonsignificant result. This can occur if the functional form of the interaction is not bilinear in nature. The traditional product term analysis is most sensitive to monotonic and uniform change in the slope as one moves across values of the moderator variable. If slope changes are not uniform, then the product term may be insensitive to the interaction. In contrast, the trichotimization procedure is sensitive to a wider array of functional forms. Although this may appear advantageous, it does not change the fact that dichotomization or trichotomization reduces precision (and subsequently statistical power) and represents a somewhat crude approach to the analysis of interaction effects. Furthermore, trichotomization can yield different patterns of results depending on what cutting scores are used to define the three groups, especially where sample sizes are modest. More efficient procedures are usually available for the analysis of complex interactions, and these are discussed in Chapter 4.

4. MORE COMPLEX INTERACTIONS

As noted in Chapter 2, the number of functional forms of an interaction effect are infinite. The traditional product term evaluates a specific type of moderated relationship, namely a bilinear interaction effect. In this chapter, we discuss procedures for testing more complex interactions through multiple regression analysis. We begin by reviewing fundamentals of analyzing nonlinear relationships using multiple regression. We then turn to the treatment of interactions between continuous variables in which the effects of an independent variable on a dependent variable are a quadratic function of the moderator variable. Next, we provide an example of nonlinear relationships with a qualitative moderator variable. A general framework for specifying interaction models in regression terms is then developed. Methods for evaluating group differences in causal models are also discussed. Finally, approaches to the exploratory analysis of interaction effects are noted.

Nonlinear Relationships in Multiple Regression: A Review

Traditional multiple regression analysis focuses on linear relationships between variables. It is possible, however, to study nonlinear relationships in the context of multiple regression. Two strategies for doing so are power polynomials and nonlinear transformations. In this section, we briefly review the basics of these two approaches. With this as background, we can then consider issues in the modeling of complex interactions.

Power Polynomials. Consider the case of a single independent variable, X, and a dependent variable, Y. A linear relationship between these two variables is expressed as follows:

$$Y = a + b_1 X + e \qquad [4.1]$$

A quadratic relationship, involving a curve with a single bend, can be modeled as follows:

$$Y = a + b_1 X + b_2 X^2 + e \qquad [4.2]$$

Figure 4.1 presents examples of quadratic relationships. A cubic relationship, involving a curve with two bends, is modeled as follows:

$$Y = a + b_1 X + b_2 X^2 + b_3 X^3 + e \qquad [4.3]$$

Figure 4.1 presents examples of cubic relationships. Curvilinear relationships are represented by the inclusion of terms that successively raise X to various powers. The number of power terms included will depend on the number of bends in the curve that are theoretically expected. For no bends (i.e., a linear relationship), X is raised to the first power. For one bend, X is raised to the second power. For two bends, X is raised to the third power, and so on. The highest order that any given equation can take is equal to $k-1$, where k is the number of distinct values of the independent variable.

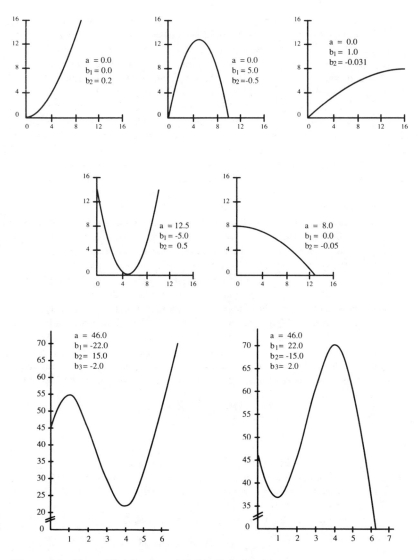

Figure 4.1. Plot of Quadratic and Cubic Relationships

To illustrate the basic logic for analyzing curvilinear relationships, consider the following example: An investigator is interested in how parenting behavior affects child development. One way in which parents differ in their upbringing of their children is the amount of independence they provide their child. Some parents encourage their children to be independent, structuring their environment in such a way that the child must frequently solve problems on his or her own. In addition, independent behaviors are highly rewarded and dependent behaviors are discouraged. Other parents develop a more dependence-oriented relationship with their child. Independent behavior is discouraged, and the child is encouraged to rely on and consult with the parent when confronted with problems. Although independent behavior is not punished, the parent rarely gives the child an opportunity for such behavior. The child is rewarded with praise and attention when seeking out the parent for assistance. In the present example, the investigator is interested in the relationship between the independence orientation of the parent and the development of cognitive skills on the part of the child. A measure of parental "independence-emphasis" that could range from 1 to 35 was obtained for each of 40 parents. Higher scores indicated that the parent emphasized independence more. A child of each parent was also tested for his or her level of cognitive skill, using a test that could range from 0 to 15. The higher the score, the more cognitive skills the child had. The investigator expected a curvilinear quadratic relationship between the two variables. Beginning with low levels of independence, the more independence the parent emphasized, the better would be the cognitive development of the child. However, at some point, too much independence would interfere with cognitive development, such that cognitive skill scores would begin to decrease with increasing levels of independence.

The investigator begins the analysis by forming two regression equations, one based on a linear model (equation 4.1) and the other based on a quadratic model (equation 4.2). In the former case, the squared multiple correlation is 0.134 while in the latter case it is 0.851. A hierarchical significance test is performed to determine if the incremental explained variance due to adding a quadratic (one-bend) term is statistically significant. Applying equation 1.3 yields the following:

$$F = \frac{(.851 - .134)/(2-1)}{(1 - .851)/(40 - 2 - 1)}$$

$$= 178.05$$

For 1 and 37 degrees of freedom, the F is statistically significant, implying that there is indeed a quadratic component to the relationship and that a simple linear model is inadequate. The strength of the quadratic effect is $0.851 - 0.134 = 0.717$, or 71.7% of the variance of cognitive skills.

The regression equation from the quadratic analysis is

$$Y + 2.524 + 0.640X + -.015X^2 + e \qquad [4.4]$$

The estimated standard errors for b_1 and b_2 are 0.044 and 0.0012, respectively. We can plot the resulting curve, by substituting a given X score into the equation and executing the calculations to yield a predicted Y score for each X. For example, if we substitute an X score of 1 into the equation, we obtain a predicted Y score of $2.524 + (.640)(1) + (-.015)(1)(1) = 3.15$. If we substitute an X score of 2 into the equation, we obtain a predicted Y score of $2.524 + (.640)(2) + (-.015)(2)(2) = 3.74$, and so on. A plot of the X scores by the predicted Y scores reveals the nature of the curve (see Figure 4.2).

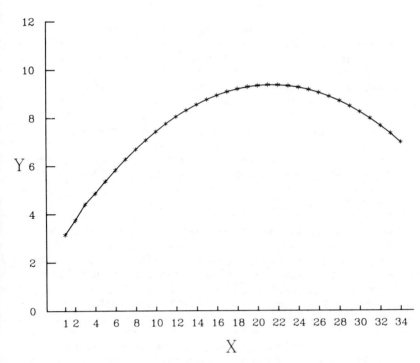

Figure 4.2. Predicted Y Scores from Quadratic Model

An alternative method for describing the curve is to identify the predicted value of Y when X is at its lowest value, the point on X where Y reaches its maximum (or minimum, in the case of a J shape), and the predicted value of Y when X is at its highest value. The point on X where Y reaches its maximum /minimum represents the value of X for which $\partial y / \partial x = 0$. It can be computed from the information in equation 4.4 using the following equation:

$$X_m = \frac{-b_1}{2b_2} = \frac{-.640}{2(-.015)} = 21.33 \qquad [4.5]$$

The predicted value of Y that occurs at this point is $2.524 + (.640) \times (21.33) + (-0.015)(21.33)(21.33) = 9.35$. The lowest score that occurred for X in the sample was 1 and the highest score was 34. Substituting these values into equation 4.4 yields predicted Y values of 3.15 and 6.94, respectively. Putting it all together, we describe the curve as follows: The relationship between parental emphasis on independence and scores on the cognitive skills test is curvilinear, as described by a quadratic equation. When parental emphasis on independence is at its lowest (1), the score on the cognitive skills test is predicted to be 3.15. As emphasis on independence increases, so do scores on the cognitive skills test, up to a point (i.e., when X scores = 21.33, test scores = 9.35). After this point, test scores begin to decrease with increasing emphasis on independence. When parental emphasis on independence is at its highest (34), the score on the cognitive skill test is predicted to decline to 6.94.

Nonlinear Transformations. Another method for testing nonlinear relationships is the use of transformations. A *linear* transformation of a variable is one that spreads scores out or contracts scores on a uniform basis, or which shifts scores up or down a numerical scale, again, uniformly. For example, if X is age and we subtract 5 years from each score obtained for a set of individuals, every score is uniformly affected. The result is a shift downward by 5 units. By contrast, a *nonlinear* transformation is one that affects the scores in a nonuniform manner. These include log transformations, power transformations, reciprocal transformations, and arcsin transformations, to name a few.

One commonly used nonlinear transformation is the log transformation. Consider the X and Y scores in section (a) of Table 4.1. There is a straightforward relationship between changes in X and changes in Y: For every one unit that X changes, Y changes by a constant proportion of the initial value of Y. For example, when X changes from 1 to 2, Y changes from 4 to 6. Note that the change of two units from 4 to 6 equals (4)(0.50). When X changes from 2 to 3, Y changes from 6 to 9. Note that the change of three units from 6 to 9 equals (6)(0.50). When X changes from 3 to 4, Y changes from 9 to 13.5. The change of 4.5 units equals (9)(0.50). In other words, for every one unit that X changes, Y changes by a proportional constant of 0.50. Sections (b) and (c) of Table 4.1 present values of X and Y for two alternative proportional constants, 0.20, and 0.80.

The relationship between X and Y in all three scenarios is clearly nonlinear in form. As the value of the proportional constant increases, a one-unit change in X is associated with progressively larger changes in Y. Although the functional form of the relationship is nonlinear, it is possible to express the relationship between Y and X in linear terms. Suppose we calculate the logarithm (to the base 10) of the Y scores. Sections (d), (e), and (f) of Table 4.1 present the transformed scores for the three data sets in (a), (b), and (c), respectively. Let us consider the data in section (d). Note that there is a linear relationship between X and log Y. For every one unit that X changes, log Y changes by 0.18 units (within rounding error). This suggests that the observed relationship between Y and X can be expressed in linear terms by means of the following equation:

$$\log Y = a + bX \qquad [4.6]$$

For the data in section (a) of Table 4.1, it can be verified that

$$\log Y = 0.42 + 0.18X \qquad [4.7]$$

Equation 4.7 can be used to obtain the original value of Y associated with any given X score. We simply substitute the value of X into the linear equation, calculate the predicted value of log Y, and then take the anti-log of this value. For example, for an X score of 2, we obtain

TABLE 4.1
Examples of Logarithmic Relationships

	Constant = 0.50			Constant = 0.20			Constant = 0.80	
(a)	Y	X	(b)	Y	X	(c)	Y	X
	4	1		4	1		4	1
	6	2		4.80	2		7.20	2
	9	3		5.76	3		12.96	3
	13.50	4		6.91	4		23.33	4
	20.25	5		8.29	5		42.00	5
	30.38	6		9.95	6		75.60	6
(d)	log Y	X	(e)	log Y	X	(f)	log Y	X
	0.60	1		0.60	1		0.60	1
	0.78	2		0.68	2		0.86	2
	0.96	3		0.76	3		1.11	3
	1.14	4		0.84	4		1.37	4
	1.32	5		0.92	5		1.63	5
	1.50	6		1.00	6		1.89	6

$$\log Y = 0.42 + (0.18)(2)$$

$$= 0.78$$

and the antilog of 0.78 is 6.0, the original value of Y.

Using versions of the above logic, it is possible to study a wide variety of nonlinear relationships within the context of a linear model. The above discussion illustrated the situation where constant additive changes in X are associated with proportional changes in Y. Other possibilities exist. For example, it might be the case that constant additive changes in Y are associated with constant proportional changes in X. This would be explored in a linear model by regressing Y onto log X. Figure 4.3 presents examples of two logarithmic functions describing this type of relationship. Or it might be the case that constant proportional changes in Y are associated with constant proportional changes in X. This would be explored in a linear model by regressing log Y onto log X, and so on. In addition, transformations other than logarithms can be used, further broadening the flexibility of the approach. Ezekiel and Fox (1959) provide a useful discussion of different transformations and their effects on measures. Complications can result in traditional regression analysis when nonlinear transformations are used. Readers interested in a more advanced treatment of this topic are referred to Draper and Smith (1981).

Effects as a Quadratic Function of a Moderator Variable

Interaction effects may not be bilinear in form and may involve complex nonlinear relationships between variables. Interactions of this nature can be

56

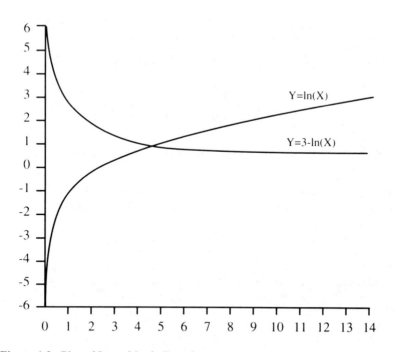

Figure 4.3. Plot of Logarithmic Functions

explored using either power polynomials or nonlinear transformations. We will now provide several illustrations.

Kenny and Judd (1984) describe a situation involving a complex interaction in the area of political behavior. The substantive issue focuses on the misperception of candidates' positions on issues. According to social psychological theory, at least two processes may underlie such misperceptions, *assimilation* and *contrast*. Assimilation occurs if voters overestimate their agreement with candidates whom they like. Contrast occurs if voters overestimate their disagreement with candidates whom they dislike. These processes predict that the relationship between a voter's position (V) on an issue and the perception of the candidate's position (C) should be moderated by the liking for the candidate (L): When an individual likes a candidate, the relationship between C and V should be positive; when an individual dislikes a candidate, the relationship between C and V should be negative.

Research in other domains has suggested that assimilation effects are more potent than contrast effects. If this is the case, then the effect of the VL interaction should be stronger at higher levels of liking: In the higher range of liking scores, changes in L should have a greater impact on the effects of V on C than in the lower range of liking scores. Table 4.2 presents hypothetical data illustrating this

TABLE 4.2

Assimilation and Contrast Example: Mean Perceived
Candidate Position as a Function of Liking and Voter Position

	Liking				
	1	2	3	4	5
Voter Position					
5	8.4	9.6	11.6	14.4	18.0
4	8.8	9.7	11.2	13.3	16.0
3	9.2	9.8	10.8	12.2	14.0
2	9.6	9.9	10.4	11.1	12.0
1	10.0	10.0	10.0	10.0	10.0
Slope	−.4	−.1	.4	1.1	2.0

phenomenon. At the lowest value of liking, the slope of C on V is −0.40. At a liking score of 2, the corresponding slope is −0.10, a change of 0.30 units (from −0.40 to −0.10) given a one-unit change in liking. At a liking score of 3, the slope of C on V is 0.40. Thus, when liking scores change one unit from 2 to 3, the slope of C on V now changes 0.50 units. Note that the change in the slope becomes progressively larger given a one-unit change in liking as one moves up the liking scale. In this case, changes in the slopes of C on V are a quadratic function of L.

The data in Table 4.2 can be modeled and evaluated by means of the following equation:

$$C = a + b_1 V + b_2 L + b_3 L^2 + b_4 VL + b_5 VL^2 + e \qquad [4.8]$$

In this model, the quadratic nature of the interaction effect is reflected in b_5. Note that this effect is evaluated in the context of "holding constant" any effects due to the main effects and the simpler bilinear interaction. Although this is not necessary in principle, it is consistent with the general strategy of focusing on unconfounded effects (see Cohen and Cohen, 1983).

The data used to generate Table 4.2 were analyzed for purposes of formally evaluating the interaction effect. The two predictors, V and L, were both centered prior to the formation of product terms. The main-effects-only model consisting of V, L and L^2 yielded a squared multiple correlation of 0.515. The squared multiple correlation for a four-term model, using the above predictors as well as the VL interaction term, yielded a squared multiple correlation of 0.714. Finally, the full five-term model described in equation 4.8 yielded a squared multiple correlation of 0.723. The test of significance of the proposed interaction effect focuses on the comparison of the three-term model with the five-term model. Using equation 1.3, we find

$$F = \frac{(.723 - .515)/(5 - 3)}{(1 - .723)/(125 - 5 - 1)}$$

$$= 44.68$$

For 2 and 119 degrees of freedom, the F is statistically significant, implying that there is an interaction effect.

The strength of the interaction effect is reflected in the difference between the respective squared multiple correlations. The interaction effect accounted for $(0.208)(100) = 20.8\%$ of the variance in the perceptions of the candidates' positions.

The nature of the interaction effect is evaluated with reference to the five-term regression equation:

$$C = 10.8 + .40V + 1.20L + .20L^2 + .60VL + .10VL^2 + e$$

All of the regression coefficients were statistically significant. The estimated standard errors for b_1 through b_5 were 0.143, 0.092, 0.077, 0.065, and 0.054, respectively. The statistically significant b_5 coefficient is consistent with the notion of stronger assimilation effects. The slope of C on V at any given value of L is computed using the same logic as discussed in previous chapters. Because the V and L scores were centered, a score on L of 0 represents the mean L score. The lowest possible centered L score is -2 (corresponding to a score of 1 on the original metric), and the highest possible centered L score is $+2$ (corresponding to a score of 5 on the original metric). As an example, to calculate the slope of C on V when the centered $L = -2$, we substitute the value of -2 wherever L occurs in the equation:

$$C = 10.8 + .40V + 1.20(-2) + .20\,(-2)^2 + .60V(-2) + .10V(-2)^2 + e$$

We then collect all terms with a V in them on the far right side:

$$C = 10.8 + 1.20(-2) + .20(-2)^2 + .40V + .60V(-2) + .10V(-2)^2 + e$$

and then we factor out V and execute the various multiplications and additions to yield

$$C = 9.2 + -0.40\,V + e$$

Performing similar calculations for the other values of L yields the following:

For centered L of -1: $C = 9.8 + -0.10V + e$

For centered L of 0: $C = 10.8 + 0.40V + e$

For centered L of 1: $C = 12.2 + 1.10V + e$

For centered L of 2: $C = 14.0 + 2.00V + e$

The standard error for any of the above slopes is computed using the formulas in Appendix A. Using equation 3.6, we can execute a test of statistical significance that contrasts any two of the slopes. It can be seen that the regression analysis adequately captures what is obvious in Table 4.2: As liking increases, the changes in slopes become increasingly larger. In this case, the effects of the independent variable on the dependent variable are quadratically related to the moderator variable.

Nonlinear Relationships and Interaction Analysis

In this section, we describe a case where the *shape* (not just the slope) of a curve changes as a function of a moderator variable. We will use an example with a qualitative moderator variable to illustrate how such variables can be incorporated into an analysis involving nonlinear relationships between continuous variables.

A communication researcher was interested in the relationship between intelligence and persuasion. She hypothesized that two fundamental processes determine how successful a communication will be in changing an individual's attitude. The first process concerns the probability that the individual will *comprehend* the communication, and the second process concerns the probability that the individual will *yield to* (or accept) the arguments of the communication once they are comprehended. Intelligence, she reasoned should be positively related to the probability of comprehending a message, but negatively related to the probability of yielding to a message. Suppose a group of individuals is presented a relatively simple message that is easy to comprehend. Under these circumstances, the major determinant of attitude change will be the probability of yielding, because comprehension is ensured for all individuals. Hence, intelligence should be negatively correlated with attitude change. Suppose a different set of individuals is provided a complex message that is moderately difficult to understand. In this case, both the probability of comprehending and the probability of yielding are relevant. Because intelligence is positively correlated with the former and negatively correlated with the latter, the resulting relationship between intelligence and attitude change should be curvilinear (representing an inverted U): Individuals who are low in intelligence should exhibit little attitude change because they are unable to comprehend the message. Individuals high in intelligence should comprehend the message, but they too will exhibit little attitude change. This is because they should be able to counterargue effectively the major points of the message, given their intelligence. Individuals who are moderately intelligent are smart enough to comprehend the message, but not smart enough to counterargue its major points. These individuals will thus be most likely to be persuaded by the message. In short, for simple communications intelligence should be negatively related to attitude change, whereas for moderately complex messages intelligence should exhibit a curvilinear relationship with attitude change.

To test this line of reasoning, the researcher administered an intelligence test to 120 individuals and then randomly assigned them to one of two conditions. In one condition, the individuals were provided a simple communication attacking an attitude that they held, whereas, in the second condition the individuals were provided a moderately complex message. The amount of attitude change induced by the respective messages was then assessed (on a 0 to 10 scale, where higher numbers indicate greater attitude change). According to the theory of the investigator, the relationship between attitude change and intelligence should be moderated by message complexity.

To analyze the data, the moderator variable of message complexity is dummy coded using the rules in Chapter 3. Because there are two levels of message complexity, only one ($k - 1 = 2 - 1$) dummy variable is required to represent group membership. All individuals in the "complex message" condition receive a score of 1 on the dummy variable, and all individuals in the "simple message" condition receive a score of 0. A power polynomial consisting of the *centered* intelligence scores (I) and the squared *centered* intelligence scores (I^2) is formed to permit the hypothesized quadratic relationship between attitude change and intelligence. The attitude change scores are then regressed onto all of these variables and their corresponding product terms in accord with the following equation:

$$Y = a + b_1 I + b_2 I^2 + b_3 D + b_4 DI + b_5 DI^2 + e$$

where D is the dummy variable representing message complexity.

The presence of an interaction effect is tested by means of a hierarchical regression analysis comparing a main-effects-only model (consisting of the terms, I, I^2, and D) and the full five-term model. The squared multiple correlation for the former was 0.262, and for the latter it was 0.540. The F test is

$$F = \frac{(.540 - .262)/(5 - 3)}{(1 - .540)/(120 - 5 - 1)}$$

$$= 34.45$$

For 2 and 114 degrees of freedom, the F is statistically significant, implying that there is an interaction effect.

The strength of the effect is indexed by the difference between the two squared multiple correlations, $0.540 - 0.262 = 0.278$. The interaction accounts for 27.8% of the variance in attitude change scores.

The nature of the interaction effect is assessed with reference to the regression equation for the full model. The equation is

$$Y = 3.868 + -.187I + (.000)I^2 + 1.740D + .209DI + -.013DI^2 + e$$

The estimated standard errors for b_1 through b_5 are 0.0198, 0.0028, 0.3398, 0.0270, and 0.0038, respectively. To discern the nature of the interaction effect, we calculate the regression curves for the two groups separately. For the complex message group, we substitute a 1 wherever D occurs:

$$Y = 3.868 + -.187I + (.000)I^2 + 1.740(1) + .209(1)I + -.013(1)I^2 + e$$

We then group the terms with I and I^2 on the right side of the equation:

$$Y = 3.868 + 1.740(1) + -.187I + .209 (1)I + (.000)I^2 + -.013(1)I^2 + e$$

and factor out I and I^2, yielding

$$Y = 5.608 + 0.22I + -0.013I^2 + e$$

To test the statistical significance of the regression coefficients associated with I and I^2, we must calculate their respective standard errors. This is accomplished with reference to the variance-covariance matrix of the regression coefficients (as provided on standard computer printout) and the formulas developed in Appendix A. For the regression coefficient associated with I, the standard error is 0.018 and the relevant t test is 0.22/0.018 = 1.22. For the regression coefficient associated with I^2, the standard error is 0.0025 and the relevant t test is −0.13/0.0025 = −5.20, $p < 0.05$. There is a statistically significant quadratic component in the equation. To describe the nature of the quadratic relationship, we use the logic developed in the context of equation 4.5: When intelligence is at its lowest point (corresponding to a centered score of −15), the predicted amount of attitude change is 2.35. As intelligence increases, so does attitude change, until intelligence equals 0.85 (or 103.6 on the original metric) and attitude change equals 5.62. After this point, increased intelligence is associated with decreases in attitude change. When intelligence is at its highest (corresponding to a centered score of 20.0), the predicted amount of attitude change is 0.85.

For the simple message group, the relevant regression equation also is computed using the above procedures. The regression equation is

$$Y = 3.868 + -.187I + (.000)I^2 + e$$

$$= 3.868 + -.187I + e$$

Because the regression coefficient for I^2 is zero, it clearly is not statistically significant.

The simple message group is best described in terms of a straightforward linear model with no quadratic component. The standard error for the regression coefficient associated with I for this group is 0.020. This yields a t value of −0.187/0.020 = −9.35, $p < 0.05$.

In sum, the relationships predicted by the theory of the investigator were borne out by the data: For the complex message, a concave downward curvilinear relationship between intelligence and attitude change was observed, whereas for simple messages, a negative linear relationship was observed.

Before leaving this example, one final set of observations should be made. As described in Chapter 3, the b_4 coefficient in the full equation represents the difference between the slopes characterizing the linear component for the two groups (i.e., the group coded 1 on the dummy variable and the reference group). The b_5 coefficient is the difference in the quadratic components for the two groups. By definition, the t tests associated with b_4 and b_5 are tests of the significance of these differences. In the current example, both of these coefficients were statistically significant. These comparisons are analogous to interaction comparisons in traditional analysis of variance paradigms.

Model Specification of Complex Interactions

In this section, we present a general system for specifying equations to evaluate complex interactions in the context of multiple regression. Consider the basic linear equation in a population:

$$Y = \alpha + BX + v \qquad [4.9]$$

where α is the population intercept, B is the population slope, and v represents an error term in the population. An interaction effect implies that the value of B varies as a function of another variable, Z. In the case of bilinear interaction, the effect of Z on B can be written in terms of a linear equation:

$$B = \beta_1 + \beta_2 Z \qquad [4.10]$$

where β_1 is an intercept term and β_2 is a slope. Note that there is no error term in equation 4.10. This implies that variations in the effect of X on Y are completely specified by Z and that other unmeasured variables do not moderate the effects of X on Y. It is possible, of course, to introduce an error term into equation 4.10. A discussion of the implications of doing so, however, is beyond the scope of this monograph because the mathematical intricacies are complex. Interested readers are referred to Mason, et al (1983).

Equations 4.9 and 4.10 can be combined by substituting $\beta_1 + \beta_2 Z$ for B

$$Y = \alpha + (\beta_1 + \beta_2 Z)X + v$$

$$= \alpha + \beta_1 X + \beta_2 XZ + v \qquad [4.11]$$

Equation 4.11 represents the model to be estimated (i.e., the *estimating model*). Parameter estimates can be derived using ordinary least squares procedures.

An alternative interaction model specifies that *both* the slope and the intercept for the regression of Y on X are moderated by Z, that is that there is a separate regression equation for each value of Z. Thus,

$$B = \beta_1 + \beta_2 Z \qquad [4.12]$$

$$\alpha = \theta_1 + \theta_2 Z \qquad [4.13]$$

Combining these equations with equation 4.9 yields

$$Y = \theta_1 + \theta_2 Z + \beta_1 X + \beta_2 XZ + v \qquad [4.14]$$

Equation 4.14 is the estimating equation. It constitutes the basic interaction model discussed in Chapters 2 and 3.

Equations 4.12 and 4.13 can be further modified to reflect yet a different interaction model that incorporates the effects of multiple moderator variables. For example,

$$B = \beta_1 + \beta_2 Z_1 + \beta_3 Z_2 \qquad [4.15]$$

$$\alpha = \theta_1 + \theta_2 Z_1 + \theta_3 Z_2 \qquad [4.16]$$

Combining these equations with equation 4.9 yields an estimating equation for the multiple interaction model discussed in Chapter 3.

It can be seen that the general method of model specification involves first specifying a base equation that represents the effects of the independent variable on the dependent variable (e.g., equation 4.9). Then, a moderator equation is specified that indicates the effects of one or more moderator variables on the slopes of the independent variable, holding all other variables constant. The basic equation and the moderator equation are then combined to yield an estimating equation. Fisher(1988) describes this approach in detail and provides several illustrations of model specification for complex interactions. For example, one common nonlinear interaction model specifies that the effect of X on Y is a multiplicative function of X, Z and an error term v, such that

$$B = \alpha X^\beta Z^\theta v \qquad [4.17]$$

When combined with equation 4.9, we obtain

$$Y = \alpha^* X^{\beta^*} Z^\theta v$$

where $\alpha^* = \alpha/(\beta + 1)$ and $\beta^* = \beta + 1$. Taking the natural logarithm of both sides yields the linear estimating equation

$$\ln Y = \ln \alpha^* + \beta^* \ln X + \theta \ln Z + \ln v \qquad [4.18]$$

Equation 4.17 represents a common model in economics and sociology. In the economics literature, it is referred to as the Cobbs-Douglas production function. The interpretation and evaluation of equations like that of the Cobbs-Douglas function involve complex issues. Interested readers are referred to Stolzenberg (1980) and Draper and Smith (1981) and the references cited therein.

The method described in this section underscores the importance of theory for the specification of interaction models: Based on a conceptual framework, the researcher derives a basic equation, a moderator equation, and an estimating equation that permits a test of the predicted interaction effects. The utility of a solid theoretical base for purposes of evaluating interaction effects cannot be emphasized strongly enough.

Interaction Analysis of Complex Causal Models

The preceding sections illustrated interaction analysis when the concern was with the relationship between a single dependent variable and a single independent variable. Frequently, an investigator will hypothesize interaction effects for entire causal structures involving multiple variables. For example, consider the causal model in Figure 4.4. According to this model, the way in which a parent acts towards his or her child influences how motivated the child is to succeed in life. This achievement motivation, in turn, influences the educational attainment of the child. Achievement motivation is also assumed to be influenced by social class, both directly and indirectly through parental behaviors. A researcher might hypothesize that the parameter values for every path in the structural model are

64

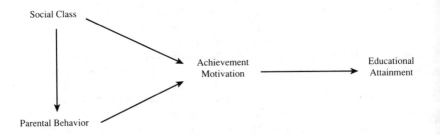

Figure 4.4. Example of a Causal Model

different for males as opposed to females. Under certain circumstances, it is possible to formally compare entire causal models, or subsets of them, for two or more groups defined by a moderator variable.

Interaction analysis in which there is an interest in contrasting multiple path coefficients for two or more groups is probably best accomplished in the context of the LISREL VII analytic framework (Jöreskog and Sörbom, 1988). LISREL uses maximum likelihood analysis to evaluate model fit for multiple groups. A causal model for any two groups can differ in two basic ways. First, the general form of the model may be different in the two groups (e.g., a path between two variables may exist for one group, but not the other). Second, although the general form might be identical (i.e., the same paths are nonzero in all groups), the values of the parameters characterizing one or more of the nonzero paths might differ between groups. A test of complete model equality between groups is obtained in LISREL by positing the same causal model for all groups and then constraining all paths to be equal in value across groups. LISREL then evaluates the overall model fit across groups. A good model fit for the overall solution suggests that the causal structures are comparable across groups. Interaction effects would predict a poor model fit across groups under such constraints. LISREL also permits the evaluation of models in which certain paths are constrained to be equal across groups and other paths are free to vary across groups. By using theory to dictate paths that should be invariant across groups vs. paths that should vary across groups, LISREL can evaluate rather complex interaction structures. The issues involved in multigroup evaluations of causal structures are well beyond the scope of this monograph. Suffice it to say that LISREL represents a powerful tool for exploring group differences in causal models. See Sörbom (1974) and Jöreskog and Sörbom (1988) for additional details.

Exploratory Analyses

On occasion, a researcher will not have a strong theory to guide the analysis of an interaction effect. However, he or she may be interested in conducting exploratory analyses to see if the data suggest the presence of an interaction. There are many approaches to conducting such exploratory analyses, including the analysis of residuals, moving averages, and nominalization. No one approach is best. Choice of a method is usually dictated by one's own preferences, given the type of statistical training that one has been exposed to.

Our own preference is to use a form of nominalization. In this approach, if either the independent variable or the moderator variable has many values, then they are first reduced to a scale with a smaller number of values (between 3 and 10). This might be accomplished, for example, by creating five subcategories of the original scale in which each category is defined by a range of values, with the ranges being equal-interval in nature. A 5 × 5 factorial table is then created in which the independent variable represents one factor, the moderator variable represents the second factor, and the relevant mean scores of the dependent variable appear in each of the 25 cells. Inspection of the means, using the principles developed in Chapter 1, will frequently suggest an interaction of a given form. Factorial plots (see Anderson, 1981) may also be applied to aid interaction specification. Additionally, one can actually execute a 5 × 5 analysis of variance and then apply the well-developed interaction decomposition methods of ANOVA (see Chapter 1). Taken together, these analyses may be most helpful in specifying an interaction form that can then be modeled using more powerful techniques.

Exploratory analyses such as these, however, must be interpreted in the context of what they are, namely post hoc data "snooping." They may be suggestive, but any conclusions must be tentative until the interaction effect is modeled and evaluated on one or more replication samples. The possibility for chance effects is substantial, especially when one considers the wide range of functional forms that can potentially occur. The more complex the interaction, the greater the danger of "over-fitting" the data. Bilinear interactions are simple and probably quite reasonable in a large number of applications. More complex interactions, in the absence of a strong theory, should be used cautiously.

5. MODERATOR ANALYSIS OF CORRELATION COEFFICIENTS

The previous chapters have examined moderated relationships from the perspective of interactive multiple regression. By definition, the focus of such an analysis is on variation in slope as a function of the moderator variable. In this chapter, we discuss issues relevant to the analysis of correlations vis-à-vis moderated relationships. We begin by discussing the conceptual differences of targeting one's analysis on correlations as opposed to slopes. Because they are highly related, we also consider issues surrounding the use of standardized and unstandardized slopes in moderator analysis. Next, we describe procedures for comparing two or more correlation coefficients from independent samples. These formulas are best suited to the case where the moderator variable is qualitative in nature. We then discuss methods of analysis when there are multiple moderator variables and/or when the moderator variable is continuous. Finally, we discuss the case of moderator analysis for dependent correlations.

Correlations versus Slopes

Moderated relationships can be characterized either in terms of correlation differences or slope differences. Consider the case where a moderator variable has two levels. An investigator can explore the moderated relationship in at least three ways, (1) by comparing the correlation between X and Y in each of the groups, (2) by comparing the unstandardized regression coefficients (based on the regression of Y onto X) in each of the groups, or (3) by comparing the standardized regression coefficients in each of the groups. In the case of the correlation coefficient, the question of interest is whether the two groups differ in the proportion of variance in Y that can be predicted from (or accounted by) X, assuming a linear model. For the case of the regression coefficients, the question of interest focuses on the extent to which *changes* in X lead to *changes* in Y differs in the two groups. These foci are quite distinct. This is most evident in the case of a simple bivariate relationship between X and Y, where the slope for Y on X is defined as follows:

$$b = r \frac{s_y}{s_x} \qquad [5.1]$$

where r is the correlation between X and Y, s_y is the standard deviation of Y and s_x is the standard deviation of X. It is evident from equation 5.1 that group differences in slopes can occur even if the correlations between X and Y are identical. Specifically, differences also might arise if the s_y are different across groups or the s_x are different across groups, or both.

Which parameter is the most appropriate one to focus on for purposes of exploring moderated relationships? The answer is that it depends on the substantive issue being explored. In general, if one is testing a causal model or evaluating how a causal relationship differs as a function of a moderator variable, then regression coefficients are the most appropriate parameters for analysis. Furthermore, unstandardized regression coefficients generally will be preferred to standardized regression coefficients. Let us explore this issue in detail.

Causal relationships typically are conceptualized in terms of change. A variable X is said to be a cause of Y if changes in X produce changes in Y. Because regression coefficients also focus on change, it is natural to study them in the context of causal models. The reason that unstandardized regression coefficients are preferred to standardized regression coefficients when comparing causal relationships in different groups centers around the concept of *causal invariance.* If a causal relationship is identical in each of a set of groups, then the coefficients on which an analysis is performed should reflect this invariance. Situations arise where unstandardized regression coefficients properly reflect causal invariance, whereas standardized regression coefficients do not. Consider a hypothetical example presented by Kim and Ferree (1981). Assume in a population that Y is completely determined by X_1 and X_2, in accord with the following linear model:

$$Y = 0.60X_1 + 0.80X_2 \qquad [5.2]$$

The value of the intercept is zero and there is no residual term. Assume also that the standard deviations of X_1 and X_2 are both 1. Now suppose that three subsets of scores are randomly selected from the population. Table 5.1 presents scores that might be observed. The scores in each group represent atypical, but nevertheless, plausible random samples. Note that each Y score is completely specified by equation 5.2. If one computes unstandardized regression coefficients in each subgroup, the result will be the generating equation (i.e., $Y = 0.60X_1 + 0.80X_2$). The coefficients are invariant. This is not true of the standardized coefficients. Specifically, the standardized coefficients for the three subgroups would be

Subset 1: $\qquad Y = 0.60X_1 + 0.80X_2 + e$

Subset 2: $\qquad Y = 0.83X_1 + 0.56X_2 + e$

Subset 3: $\qquad Y = 0.35X_1 + 0.94X_2 + e$

These coefficients are not invariant across subgroups (or over replications of experiments) and do not adequately reflect the generating causal function. Given an invariant causal structure, unstandardized regression coefficients are capable of detecting that invariance, while standardized regression coefficients are not. This is true even when the structural coefficients in the population are assumed to be standardized in form (see Kim and Ferree, 1981, for a more elaborate discussion of the issues involved). Thus, unstandardized coefficients are generally preferred to standardized ones.

Although researchers interested in testing causal models focus on regression coefficients, there are situations where one will want to compare correlation coefficients across groups. For example, organizational psychologists and educational researchers frequently are interested in determining whether a test is equally valid in two or more groups. Using traditional psychometric theory, a validity coefficient is defined as the correlation between the test in question and an external criterion. In this case, there is no concern with causal relations. Rather, the issue is whether the validity coefficients differ across groups. For example, the differential validity of intelligence tests for blacks and whites in the United States has been extensively investigated.

Chapters 2 through 4 discussed in detail methods for analyzing differences in slopes as a function of moderator variables. In this chapter, we present methods for analyzing differences in correlation coefficients as a function of a moderator variable.

TABLE 5.1

Example of Three Subsets from a Population

	Subgroup 1			Subgroup 2			Subgroup 3		
Individual	Y	X_1	X_2	Y	X_1	X_2	Y	X_1	X_2
1	1.4	1	1	2.0	2	1	2.2	1	2
2	−0.2	1	−1	0.4	2	−1	−1.0	1	−2
3	0.2	−1	1	−0.4	−2	1	1.0	−1	2
4	−1.4	−1	−1	−2.0	−2	−1	−2.2	−1	−2

Analysis of the Difference Between Independent Correlations

Test of Significance. Consider a case where the moderator variable is qualitative in nature and we want to compare the correlation between X and Y for each group defined by the moderator variable. The null hypothesis is that all of the population correlations are equal. The alternative hypothesis is that they are not all equal. The evaluation of the null hypothesis requires that we transform each correlation to Fisher's Z, via the formula

$$Z = 0.5[\ln(1 + r) - \ln(1 - r)] \qquad [5.3]$$

where r is the correlation between X and Y in a given group, Z is the value of the transformed r, and ln is the natural logarithm. The various Zs are then combined by means of the following formula:

$$Q = \Sigma (n_j - 3)(Z_j - Z')^2 \qquad [5.4]$$

where n_j is the number of observations for group j and the summation is performed across all groups, and

$$Z' = \Sigma w_j Z_j \qquad [5.5]$$

$$w_j = \frac{n_j - 3}{\Sigma (n_j - 3)} \qquad [5.6]$$

Q is approximately distributed as a chi-square with $k-1$ degrees of freedom. A common two-group version of equation 5.4 uses the normal distribution as the sampling distribution:

$$z = \frac{Z_1 - Z_2}{[(n_1 - 3)^{-1} + (n_2 - 3)^{-1}]^{1/2}} . \qquad [5.7]$$

If the null hypothesis is rejected when there are more than two groups, then the researcher may wish to conduct selected pairwise comparisons of correlations, to elucidate the source of the effect. This introduces the problem of inflated experimentwise error rates. If appropriate, protection from such Type I errors can be introduced, although the optimal procedure for doing so is somewhat controversial. One approach uses an adjusted Bonferroni procedure (Holland and Copenhaver, 1988). Each of the pairwise contrasts of interest is executed using equation 5.7. The p value associated with each resulting z is obtained from tables of the standard normal distribution. The p values are then ordered from smallest to largest that is from 1 to k. Tied p are ordered arbitrarily. Let i be the rank order of the p value in question. A contrast is declared as being statistically significant if the p value associated with the contrast is less than

$$\frac{\alpha}{k - i + 1} \qquad [5.8]$$

where α is the per comparison error rate (traditionally 0.05). This form of the Bonferroni test is statistically more powerful than the traditional Bonferroni method, but it still is a somewhat conservative procedure (see Holm, 1979).

As an example, suppose that an investigator is interested in comparing the validity coefficients (in the form of correlations) of an intelligence test for three groups of individuals: whites, blacks, and Hispanics. There are 100 individuals in each group, and the observed correlations are 0.82, 0.63, and 0.56, respectively. The Z transforms are 1.16, 0.74, and 0.63. The weights for each Z are calculated using equation 5.6 and they equal 0.33, 0.33, and 0.33, respectively. Z' is determined to be 0.84, and

$$Q = (100 - 3)(1.16 - 0.84)^2 + (100 - 3)(0.74 - 0.84)^2$$
$$+ (100 - 3)(0.63 - 0.84)^2$$
$$= 15.17$$

For two degrees of freedom, Q is statistically significant, and the null hypothesis of equal validity coefficients is rejected. To apply the Bonferroni-based procedure, the z scores comparing all possible pairs of correlations are computed using equation 5.7. For the contrast between whites and blacks, the z is 2.92 and the associated p value is 0.0018. For the contrast between whites and Hispanics, the z is 3.69 and the associated p value is 0.0001. For the contrast between whites and blacks, the z is 0.77 and the associated p value is 0.2206. The p values are ordered as follows:

Value of i	p value	$\alpha/(k - i + 1)$
1	0.0001	0.017
2	0.0018	0.025
3	0.2206	0.050

Based on the above, we conclude that the validity coefficient for whites differs significantly from the validity coefficients for both blacks and Hispanics. However, the validity coefficients for the latter two groups are not significantly different.

Statistical Power. Methods for statistical power analysis of Q in equation 5.4 are described by Cohen (1988). To gain some insight into power considerations, Table 5.2 presents sample sizes that are necessary to reject the null hypothesis when comparing correlation coefficients for two groups, for $\alpha = 0.05$ (two-tailed), assuming an equal number of individuals in the two groups. The columns of the table represent population differences between Z transformed correlations. The cell entries represent the approximate sample size, per group, that is required to achieve the level of power specified in the entry on the far left of the row. For example, if the Z score difference in the population is 0.30, then the number of individuals in each of the two groups must be 177 to achieve power of 0.80. As another example, if one conducts an investigation with 195 individuals per group, and the population difference between the Z transforms is 0.20, then the power of the statistical test will be 0.50. In other words, only half of the time will the researcher correctly reject the null hypothesis; for the other half, the researcher will be discouraged from pursuing a potentially interesting moderator effect. Table 5.2 makes explicit that the sample sizes necessary to detect small to moderate differences in correlations is rather substantial, by the standards of most social science research.

Analysis of Correlations Using the General Linear Model

The methods described in the preceding section are most applicable when there is a single moderator variable and when there are few groups defined by the moderator variable. It is possible to analyze correlations as a function of multiple moderator variables and/or as a function of a multivalued continuous moderator variable. The technique is based on the general linear model and is described by Hedges and Olkin (1985). To apply the procedure, the Z transforms of the relevant correlation coefficients are treated as a criterion variable, and the moderator variables are treated as predictor variables. A multiple regression analysis is performed regressing the Z transforms onto the moderator variables. Because the sample sizes for each correlation may differ, a *case-weight* regression analysis is performed, where the weight of a given case is $n - 3$. Case-weight regression analysis is available on many computer packages (e.g., SPSS-X, SAS Proc GLM). The test of overall model fit uses a statistic, Q_E, that is approximately distributed as chi-square with $j - k$ degrees of freedom, where j is the number of correlation coefficients and k is the number of moderator variables. The mathematical rationale and development of Q_E is described in Hedges and Olkin (1985). The statistic is identical to the weighted "error sum of squares" about the regression

TABLE 5.2

Sample Sizes Needed to Attain Selected Levels of Statistical Power

	Population difference between Z								
	0.10	0.20	0.30	0.40	0.50	0.60	0.70	0.80	1.00
Power									
0.25	333	86	40	24	16	12	10	8	6
0.50	771	195	88	51	34	24	19	15	11
0.60	983	248	112	64	42	30	23	18	13
0.70	1237	312	140	80	52	37	28	22	15
0.80	1573	395	177	101	66	47	35	28	19
0.85	1799	452	203	115	75	53	40	31	21
0.90	2104	528	236	134	87	61	46	36	24
0.95	2602	653	292	165	107	75	56	44	29

line, which is provided on computer output for case-weight regression analysis. A model is said to be misspecified if Q_E is statistically significant. Note that this is the reverse of the typical hypothesis testing situation, where statistical significance usually implies some degree of model fit. The test of the null hypothesis — that a given regression coefficient for a moderator variable is zero — is executed by dividing the square of the coefficient by its corresponding diagonal element in what is commonly referred to as the $\mathbf{X'WX}$ inverse matrix, also provided on standard computer printout. The resulting statistic is distributed as a chi-square with one degree of freedom.

As an example, Hedges and Olkin (1985) examine the correlation between scores on a reasoning task and scores on an aptitude test for males and females in each of three grade levels. Table 5.3 presents the data. Gender and grade level were conceptualized as moderator variables. Both variables were dummy coded. Taken together, there were four dummy variables, one for the grand mean, one for gender, and two for grade level. The Z scores were regressed onto the relevant dummy variables using case-weighted multiple regression. The underlying model stated that variations in the correlations could be explained in terms of an additive combination of the two moderator variables. The observed Q_E statistic was 3.91 and is compared with a critical value of 5.99 (based on $6 - 4 = 2$ degrees of freedom). The results are consistent with correct model specification. The only significant regression coefficient was that for the grand mean. This suggests that the correlations, as a group, are different from zero, but that there are no appreciable gender or grade effects.

The approach of Hedges and Olkin (1985) is useful because it can be extended to include models that incorporate interactions between moderated variables as determinants of the correlation between two variables. In addition, it can be applied to the case of continuous moderator variables. For more details, see Hedges and Olkin (1985).

TABLE 5.3

General Linear Model Example

Grade	Gender	Sample Size	r	Z
7	Male	145	0.19	0.19
7	Female	159	−0.08	−0.08
9	Male	136	0.31	0.32
9	Female	77	0.10	0.10
11	Male	122	0.16	0.16
11	Female	139	0.21	0.21

Analysis of the Difference Between Dependent Correlations

On rare occasions, an investigator may want to explore a moderated relationship for dependent correlations. For example, one might hypothesize that the validity coefficient for X and Y is different at time 1 than at time 2, where X and Y are assessed on the *same* individuals at two points in time. In this case, time is viewed as a moderator variable with two levels. The relevant statistical test to compare the correlations is described by Kenny (1979:239). Let variable 1 = X at time 1, variable 2 = X at time 2, variable 3 = Y at time 1, and variable 4 = Y at time 2. The correlation between X at time 1 and X at time 2 is denoted as $r_{1\,2}$, the correlation between X at time 1 and Y at time is denoted as $r_{1\,3}$, the correlation between X at time 2 and Y at time 2 is denoted as $r_{2\,4}$, and so on. Then

$$z = \frac{N^{1/2}(r_{1\,3} - r_{2\,4})}{\left[(1 - r_{1\,4}{}^2)^2 + (1 - r_{2\,3}{}^2)^2 - c\right]^{1/2}} \qquad [5.9]$$

where

$$c = (r_{1\,2} - r_{2\,3}r_{1\,3})(r_{3\,4} - r_{2\,4}r_{3\,4}) + (r_{1\,4} - r_{1\,2}r_{2\,4})(r_{2\,3} - r_{1\,2}r_{1\,3})$$

$$+ (r_{1\,2} - r_{1\,4}r_{2\,4})(r_{3\,4} - r_{1\,3}r_{1\,4}) + (r_{1\,4} - r_{1\,3}r_{3\,4})(r_{2\,3} - r_{3\,4}r_{2\,4})$$

and N refers to the number of individuals. z has approximately a standard normal distribution and can be evaluated for statistical significance using tables of the standard normal distribution. Extension of equation 5.9 to three or more levels of the moderator variable is complex.

6. METHODOLOGICAL AND SUBSTANTIVE ISSUES

Interaction effects are relevant to a wide range of disciplines in the social sciences. This is evident, in part, from the varied examples that we used throughout this monograph. In this chapter we offer some general observations about interaction analysis, based on applications in substantive domains.

"False" Interaction Effects

It is possible to observe an interaction effect in a set of sample data when no such interaction effect exists in the population. This, of course, is referred to as a Type I error and, within the context of statistical theory, should occur only with a probability equal to one's alpha level. However, independent of statistical theory, there are aspects of methodology and research design that can also lead to misleading conclusions about the presence of interaction effects. We have alluded to some of these issues in previous chapters, such as the problem of conducting interaction analysis with ordinal level measures. In this section, we will briefly discuss additional factors that can produce interaction effects in a set of data, but whose substantive significance is trivial (i.e., the effect is artifactual).

The issues can be illustrated with reference to a domain where interaction analysis has received considerable attention, namely personnel psychology. This branch of psychology spends considerable conceptual and empirical effort on the development of tests that will forecast the performance of employees and that will help an employer place an employee in the right type of position. Personnel psychologists are concerned about test validity and the extent to which a test is applicable across a wide range of populations and situations. When validity coefficients are found to vary across groups or conditions, then limitations are placed on the test accordingly.

Moderator research in personnel psychology tends to explore moderated relationships in the context of correlation coefficients rather than regression coefficients. When regression coefficients are examined, more often than not the focus is on standardized as opposed to unstandardized slopes. We believe that many applications in this area should be studied, instead, with unstandardized regression coefficients. Nevertheless, there are legitimate research questions in this area that appropriately focus on variations in correlations.

Group differences in correlations (and standardized regression coefficients) can occur for many reasons, some of which are artifactual in nature. When an interaction effect or a moderated relationship is the result of a substantively irrelevant factor, then it is termed a *false* moderator. For example, two groups may exhibit different correlations between X and Y because in one group there is a restricted range (i.e., less variability in X or Y) relative to the other group. If the restricted range is the result of arbitrary sampling decisions, then the observed interaction effect/moderated relationship is a false one. Personnel psychologists have developed numerous procedures for dealing with range restriction problems to reduce the threat of a false moderator (e.g., Alliger, 1987; Alliger and Alexander, 1988). Other factors that may induce false moderators include (a) group differences in the reliability of the criterion variable, (b) group differences in the reliability of the predictor variables, (c) group differences in criterion contamination (see Brogden and Taylor, 1950), (d) group differences in the predictor variable metric (see Jaccard and Dittus, 1990; Kim and Ferree, 1981), and (e) group differences in the criterion variable metric, to name a few.

False moderators are system dependent. What is deemed a false moderator in one theoretical framework may be deemed a true moderator in another theoretical framework. False moderators must be evaluated in the context of the entire research process, including the conceptual system, the research design, the measurement of variables, and the sampling of individuals.

Moderator analysis in personnel psychology sometimes relies on the comparison of correlations across studies as opposed to groups. For example, two studies might be reported in the literature, one that observes a statistically significant correlation between X and Y and one that does not. The scientist reviewing the literature may conclude that a moderated relationship exists, and may then speculate on study differences that are the source of the moderator effect. Such a situation is highly susceptible to false moderators. The major problem is that a direct test of the difference between the correlations is never executed. Suppose that two studies used the same sample size, and that one study observed a correlation of 0.35, which was just barely statistically significant, while the other study observed a correlation of 0.33, which did not achieve statistical significance. One would be hard-pressed to argue that a moderator relationship exists, because the *difference* between the two correlations is clearly trivial. The logic is even more clouded when studies vary in sample size and hence in their statistical power. Two studies might observe an identical correlation coefficient, yet in one study it may be deemed statistically significant whereas in another study it is not, purely because of the differences in sample size and the consequent effect on statistical power. Moderator analysis requires a direct test of the differences between correlations or slopes.

Failure To Detect Interaction Effects

In many areas of inquiry, interaction effects have failed to manifest themselves, even when they are predicted on the basis of common sense or a strong theory. Thus, another problem in interaction analysis is the failure to detect interaction effects that do, indeed, exist. We believe that there are several reasons why true interaction effects may go undetected. Most of these reasons have already been discussed in previous chapters. They include problems related to multicollinearity, measurement error, inappropriate metrics, small sample sizes, and model misspecification. To counteract these problems, we make five recommendations.

1. To reduce potential problems with multicollinearity, the X variables should be centered prior to the formation of product terms.

2. Efforts should be made to maximize the reliability of the measures involved in the analysis. Methodological procedures for reducing measurement error are discussed by Anderson (1982), and Wegenar (1982). If an interaction term predicted by a strong theory is not statistically significant and fallible measures are present, then one should consider the possibility of using either a multiple indicator approach (e.g., Kenny and Judd, 1984)

or the correction approaches based on Heise (1986) and others. Each of these approaches, however, has limitations associated with it.

3. Researchers should adopt methodological practices that promote equal interval characteristics of their measurement scales. Such practices are discussed by Anderson (1982) and Wegenar (1982). If departures from intervality are likely to be large, then moderated regression analysis may be inappropriate. At a minimum, any observed interactions under such conditions must yield theoretically meaningful interpretations and should be replicated in other research with alternative measurement methods.

4. Researchers should ensure that their sample size is large enough to achieve adequate levels of statistical power.

5. The functional form of the interaction should be considered on an a priori basis. If the form is not bilinear, then a traditional crossproduct term is inappropriate for evaluating the interaction effect. Appropriate nonlinear modeling methods should then be used to introduce terms that are representative of the hypothesized interaction. In the absence of a strong theory, preliminary exploratory methods may reveal the functional form of the interaction that should be pursued.

Ordinal and Disordinal Interactions

Social scientists distinguish between *ordinal* interaction effects and *disordinal* interaction effects. The distinctions are usually made in the context of qualitative moderator variables consisting of two or three groups. A disordinal interaction is one in which the regression line for one group intersects with the regression line for the other group. This is also referred to as a *crossover* interaction. An ordinal interaction is one in which the regression lines are nonparallel, but they do not intersect. Figure 6.1 presents an example of a disordinal and ordinal interaction.

The concept of ordinal-disordinal interaction has been important in numerous substantive domains. For example, Cronbach and Gleser (1957) review the logic of classification decisions in educational, organizational, and psychological research. These authors note that decisions about the assignment of people to treatments (e.g., clinical interventions, type of educational curricula, type of job) are frequently guided by the identification of crossover points in disordinal interactions: Persons to the right of the crossover point are assigned to one treatment, while persons to the left of the crossover point are assigned to the other treatment condition. In contrast, ordinal interactions imply the same treatment should be used for all individuals.

Statisticians have expressed some wariness about ordinal interactions. Such interactions, they contend, may be an artifact of the metric of the dependent variable. Nonparallel regression lines frequently can be made parallel by means of a monotonic transformation of the Y scores. If the metric intervals of Y are truly arbitrary, then it makes sense from the standpoint of scientific parsimony to perform such transformations and remove the false moderator. Ordinal interactions, however, should not be dismissed if their metrics are meaningful. As Cronbach and Snow (1981) demonstrate, such interactions can be substantively important and, when coupled with cost-benefit criteria, can be crucial for classification decisions.

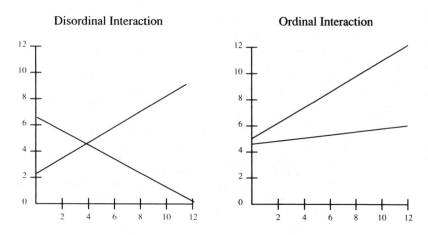

Figure 6.1. Example of an Ordinal and Disordinal Interaction

For any given pair of nonparallel regression lines, there is always a point where the lines will intersect. In this sense, all interactions are disordinal in character. Interactions are classified as being ordinal if, *within the range of scores being studied* (e.g., for IQ scores between 90 and 110), the regression lines do not intersect. Consider the case where the moderator consists of two groups and the investigator is studying the relationship between a dependent variable Y and an independent variable X. It is possible to identify the point on X where the regression lines for the two groups intersect using the following formula:

$$P_I = \frac{a_1 - a_2}{b_2 - b_1} \qquad [6.1]$$

where a_1 is the intercept for the first group, a_2 is the intercept for the second group, b_1 = the slope for the first group, and b_2 = the slope for the second group. As an illustration, consider the following example: A consumer psychologist is interested in the relationship between perceived cost of a product and the attitude toward the product. The relationship between these variables is studied for two groups of individuals: (1) a group of relatively poor, urban, lower-class individuals, and (2) a group of affluent, young, urban professionals. The investigator believes that perceived cost is differentially related to product attitudes in the two groups. For the lower-class sample, increasing cost of the product should have a negative impact on the attitude toward the product. This is because such individuals would find it more difficult to purchase the product given increased cost. For the more affluent sample, the reverse is predicted: Increasing the cost of the product will have a positive effect on the attitude toward the product. This is because a higher cost product is associated with more status and higher product quality, without placing a burden on the economic constraints of the individual. In this study there were 20 individuals in each group. A measure of perceived cost was obtained by asking the individual to estimate how many dollars the product cost. The attitude toward the product was measured on a seven-point semantic differential scale, with higher scores implying a more positive attitude.

To analyze the data, group membership was dummy coded using a single dummy vector. The attitude scores were then regressed onto the perceived cost scores, the dummy variable, and the product of these two variables. The interaction effect was highly significant, and the regression equations for the two groups were as follows:

More affluent: $Y = 1.193 + 0.098X + e$

Less affluent: $Y = 7.193 + -0.107X + e$

The slopes were in the predicted direction and differed significantly from each other ($p < 0.05$). A plot of the scores and the regression lines revealed that the interaction was disordinal in character. The point of intersection is

$$P_I = \frac{1.193 - 7.193}{-0.107 - 0.098} = 29.27$$

This point describes the score on X where the predicted attitudes are the same for the two groups. Thus, when the product is perceived to cost $29.27, the attitudes of less affluent people are identical to the attitudes of more affluent people. As the perceived cost exceeds $29.27, the attitudes of more affluent people diverge by becoming increasingly more positive relative to less affluent people. As the perceived cost decreases from a value of $29.27, the attitudes of more affluent people diverge by becoming increasingly more negative to less affluent people.

Johnson-Neyman Analysis. Johnson and Neyman (1936) develop a method that enables the researcher to establish "regions of nonsignificance" relevant to the interpretation of the interaction effect. Researchers who decompose disordinal interaction effects find this analysis to be informative. The approach defines a range of scores on the X variable where the Y scores of the two groups do not differ significantly (as defined by an a priori defined alpha level). For example, in the present data a Johnson-Neyman analysis yielded a region of nonsignificance, based on an alpha of 0.05, defined by the values of $27.36 and $31.07. This means that individuals whose perceived cost fell within the range of $27.36 and $31.07 did not differ significantly in their attitudes toward the product. When perceived cost exceeded $31.07, then more affluent individuals were more positive in their attitudes than less affluent individuals. When perceived cost was less than $27.36, then more affluent individuals were more negative in their attitudes than less affluent people. These "confidence limits" help the researcher to appreciate the strength of the interaction effect.

Johnson-Neyman values are obtained by solving for the two values of X that satisfy the following formula (Kerlinger and Pedhazur, 1973):

$$X = \frac{-B \pm (B^2 - AC)^{1/2}}{A} \qquad [6.2]$$

To define the values of A, B, and C, let N = the total number of subjects, n_1 = the number of individuals in group 1, n_2 = the number of individuals in group 2, F_α = a tabled F ratio with 1 and $N - 4$ degrees of freedom that corresponds to the experimenter-defined alpha level (traditionally 0.05), M_1 = the mean score on X for group 1, M_2 = the mean score on X for group 2, S_1 = the sum of squared deviations for X for group 1, S_2 = the sum of squared deviations for X for group 2, and E = the residual sum of squares from the overall analysis. Then

$$A = \frac{-F_\alpha}{N-4} E \frac{1}{S_1} + \frac{1}{S_2} + (b_1 - b_2)^2$$

$$B = \frac{F_\alpha}{N-4} E \frac{M_1}{S_1} + \frac{M_2}{S_2} + (a_1 - a_2)(b_1 - b_2)$$

$$C = \frac{-F_\alpha}{N-4} E \frac{N}{n_1 n_2} + \frac{M_1^2}{S_1} + \frac{M_2^2}{S_2} + (a_1 - a_2)^2$$

Extensions of the Johnson-Neyman technique to more than two groups and more than one continuous variable may be found in Johnson and Fay (1950), Johnson and Jackson (1959), Potthoff (1964), and Walker and Lev (1953). The approach is also applicable to the analysis of ordinal interactions, as discussed in the above references. Cronbach and Snow (1981) have reviewed the strengths and limitations of the Johnson-Neyman approach. Alternative approaches have been suggested by Aitkin (1973), Potthoff (1964), and Wunderlich and Borich (1973).

Concluding Comments

We have introduced a wide range of concepts and issues in the analysis of interaction effects involving continuous variables. We would like to emphasize the following points from our treatment. Most importantly, interaction analysis is most straightforward when it is theoretically motivated; theory guides the specification of appropriate interaction models using multiple regression. Traditional product terms with continuous variables assess interaction of a specific form, namely bilinear interactions. Other functional forms may be dictated by theory, and many of these forms can be modeled within a regression context. When conducting interaction analysis, we have found it useful to organize our analysis around three fundamental questions: (1) Given the sample data, can we infer that an interaction effect exists in the population, (2) if so, what is the strength of the effect, and (3) if so, what is the nature of the effect? When formulating research to test for interaction effects, one should consider issues related to sample size (for purposes of power analysis), levels of measurement, measurement error, potential multicollinearity, and other methodological/substantive issues discussed above. We believe that social scientists who work with structural equation models and correlational data can benefit greatly by thinking about potential interaction effects in the context of their theories and models. Unfortunately, as documented in Chapter 1, the tendency has been to omit such effects in many cases where they are plausible.

In concluding our treatment of interaction effects, we provide the reader with a list of ten empirical applications that have used multiple regression for the analysis of moderated relationships. These can be read to gain an appreciation of the many forms that interaction analysis takes. The relevant articles are Cleary (1968) Etzion (1984) Feris, Bergin, and Wayne (1988), Follette and Jacobson (1987), LaRocco, House, and French (1980), Link (1987), Oldham and Fried (1987), Phillips and Freedman (1985), Rothman (1974), and Zika and Chamberlin (1987). We have found the following journals to be particularly useful in keeping abreast of analytic developments in interaction analysis: *Journal of Applied Psychology, Psychological Bulletin, Sociological Methods and Research,* and *Organizational Behavior and Human Decision Processes.*

APPENDIX A
Computation of Standard Errors

This appendix describes the equation for calculating the standard error of the slope of Y on X_1 at given values of X_2 and X_3. The equation is applicable to the derivation of regression coefficients in three-way interaction models vis-à-vis equation 3.4. This equation reveals that four regression coefficients from the generating equation are used in the derivation of the slope in question, b_1, b_4, b_5, and b_7. The formula for calculating the relevant standard error uses the variances and covariances of each of these coefficients, which are obtained on standard computer output. Let

$$A = \text{var}(b_1) + X_2^2 \text{var}(b_4) + X_3^2 \text{var}(b_5) + X_2^2 X_3^2 \text{var}(b_7)$$

$$B = 2X_2 \text{cov}(b_1, b_4) + 2X_3 \text{cov}(b_1, b_5)$$

$$C = 2X_2 X_3 \text{cov}(b_4, b_5) + 2X_2 X_3 \text{cov}(b_1, b_7)$$

$$D = 2X_2^2 X_3 \text{cov}(b_4, b_7) + 2X_2 X_3^2 \text{cov}(b_5, b_7),$$

Then, using standard logic for the combination of variances (see Kmenta, 1986), the relevant standard error for the slope of Y on X_1 at the given values of X_2 and X_3 is

$$s[b \text{ at } (X_2, X_3)] = (A + B + C + D)^{1/2}.$$

For equations involving power terms, as discussed in Chapter 4, the logic is similar. For example, in the problem on perceptions of candidate positions, we calculated the slope of the perceived candidate's position (Y) on the voter's own position (V) at different values of liking (L). The calculation of the slope used b_1, b_4, and b_5 from the generating equation. We therefore require the variances and covariances of these three coefficients to calculate the relevant standard error. Let

$$A = \text{var}(b_1) + L^2 \text{var}(b_4) + L^2 L^2 \text{var}(b_5)$$

$$B = 2L \text{cov}(b_1, b_4) + 2L^2 \text{cov}(b_1, b_5)$$

$$C = 2L(L^2) \text{cov}(b_4, b_5),$$

Then the relevant standard error for the slope of Y on X_1 at the given value of L is

$$s(b \text{ at } L) = (A + B + C)^{1/2}.$$

The second example in Chapter 4 used dummy variables in which a quadratic equation was calculated in each of two groups based on a generating equation with five predictor variables. In this example, Y refers to the dependent variable (attitude change), I refers to the independent variable (intelligence), and D refers to the dummy variable representing group membership. To calculate the slope of Y on I for the group coded 1, we use b_1 and b_4 from the generating equation. The standard error is thus

$$s(I \text{ at } D = 1) = \left[\text{var}(b_1) + D^2 \text{var}(b_4) + 2D \text{cov}(b_1, b_4) \right]^{1/2}$$

$$= \left[\text{var}(b_1) + (1)^2 \text{var}(b_4) + 2(1) \text{cov}(b_1, b_4) \right]^{1/2}$$

Calculation of the standard error for the other values of D involves simple substitution of the value of D into the equations. The standard error for the slope of Y on I^2 is obtained by using the appropriate variances and covariances for b_2 and b_5 in place of b_1 and b_2.

APPENDIX B
Computer Programs

This appendix presents a set of programs written in BASIC that compute several of the statistics discussed in this monograph. The programs are intended to supplement the use of standard statistical packages, such as SPSS-X, BMDP, and SAS, and perform further analyses on output derived from these programs. The programs were written to maximize generalizability across different versions of BASIC. Hence, they are not always efficient. The version of BASIC that was used to develop the programs was QuickBasic 4.0. However, with a few minor exceptions, all programs should execute on most forms of BASIC.

Versions of BASIC differ in the following ways (as they pertain to the programs): First, the command CLS is used in QuickBasic to clear the screen. Some versions of BASIC use a different command. Second, INPUT statements solicit user responses with a short phrase contained within quotations, followed by a comma and a variable name. Some versions of BASIC use a semicolon instead of a comma, and a single quote (') instead of a double quote ("). Third, the square root function is executed using the call function SQR. Some versions of BASIC use SQRT. Fourth, a single command has been placed at the beginning of the program so that the letters appear in green. For users with monochrome monitors, this statement should be omitted. Other versions of BASIC may use a different command structure to manipulate color. Finally, blank PRINT statements have been added in places to make the presentation more aesthetically pleasing. Depending on your system, these statements may not be necessary. Aside from these differences, the programs should be compatible with a wide variety of BASIC.

There are six programs, linked together by a central index. Each program is selfcontained and can be used independently of the other programs. Thus, it is possible to enter the code for only a subset of the programs, if that is desired. For each program, an example is provided together with the results of the analysis. This can be used to verify whether the entry of the program has been successful.

If the entry is correct, then the results provided in the example should be obtained. If the programs are verified against the examples provided in Chapters 1 through 6, then small discrepancies in answers may be observed due to rounding error. When performing calculations in these chapters, we frequently rounded to two or three decimal places, in the interest of pedagogy. The BASIC programs are considerably more precise, and the discrepancies may be moderate in size when the operations involve square roots and division of very small numbers.

Hierarchical Multiple Regression. This program executes equation 1.3. To test if program entry is correct, use the following example: Multiple R for the original equation = 0.30; multiple R for the expanded equation = 0.60; number of predictors in the original equation = 2; number of predictors in the expanded equation = 3; total sample size = 300. The results should yield an incremental R^2 of 0.27, an F of 124.875 with 1 and 296 degrees of freedom.

Interaction Analysis with One-Product Term. This program executes follow-up analyses for traditional product terms involving continuous variables, as discussed in Chapter 2. Let Y be the dependent variable, X_1 be the independent variable, and X_2 be the moderator variable. The program calculates the intercept and slope for the linear regression of Y onto X_1 at any given value of X_2. In addition, the standard error for the slope is computed as well as a t test for statistical significance. Analyses using dummy variables are not permissible (except for cases where there is a single dummy vector) because of the wide array of designs that are potentially relevant.

As a test example, use the following: Value of X_2 to evaluate = 3, $a = -1$, $b_1 = 6$, $b_2 = 1$, $b_3 = -1$, var(b_1) = 0.04545, var(b_3) = 0.00413, cov(b_1, b_3) = $-.01240$, $N = 125$. Results should yield an intercept of 2.0, a slope of 3.0, a standard error of 0.09066, and a t of 33.089 with 121 degrees of freedom.

Interaction Analysis for a Three-Way Product Term. This program evaluates the intercept and slope for Y on X_1 at specified values of X_2 and X_3, as discussed in Chapter 3. To test the accuracy of program entry, use the following example: Value of X_2 to evaluate = 5, value of X3 to evaluate = 10, $N = 300$, $a = 2$, $b_1 = 1$, $b_2 = 3$, $b_3 = 2.5$, $b_4 = 1.5$, $b_5 = 0.5$, $b_6 = 3.5$, $b_7 = 4$, var(b_1) = 0.02, var(b_4) = 0.03, var(b_5) = 0.04, var(b_7) = 0.03. Set all requested covariances equal to 0.001. Results should yield an intercept of 217, a slope of 213.5, a standard error of 9.028, and a t of 23.649 with 292 degrees of freedom.

Interaction Analysis for Quadratic Effects. This program calculates the intercept and slope of Y on X_1 at specified values of X_2 when slope changes are assumed to be a quadratic function of X_2. This form of analysis was discussed in Chapter 4. To test the accuracy of code entry, use the following example: Value of X_2 to evaluate = -2, $N = 125$, $a = 10.8$, $b_1 = 0.4$, $b_2 = 1.2$, $b_3 = 0.2$, $b_4 = 0.6$, $b_5 = 0.1$, var(b_1) = 0.0006, var(b_4) = 0.0001, var(b_5) = 0.00009. Set all requested covariances equal to zero, except cov(b_1, b_5). Let cov(b_1, b_5) = -0.0002. Results should yield an intercept of 9.2, a slope of -0.4, a standard error of 0.02898, and a t of -13.801 with 119 degrees of freedom.

Test of the Difference Between Independent Correlations. This program calculates a test of significance for the difference between two or more independent correlations. In the case of two correlations, a z statistic is computed. In the case of three or more correlations, a chi-square statistic is computed. To test the accuracy of your program entry, use the following example: Compare three correlations. The sample sizes are each 100. The correlations are 0.82, 0.63, and 0.56. The results should yield a chi-square of 14.838 with 2 degrees of freedom.

Test of the Difference Between Dependent Correlations. This program calculates a test of significance for the difference two dependent correlations, as described in Chapter 5. To test the accuracy of your code entry, use the following example: To examine the difference between the correlation of X and Y at time 1 with the correlation of X and Y at time 2, enter the following: N = 300, r X_1 with X_2 = 0.65, r X_1 with Y_1 = 0.41, r X_1 with Y_2 = 0.44, r X_2 with Y_1 = 0.26, r X_2 with Y_2 = 0.37, r Y_1 with Y_2 = 0.71. The resulting test comparing the differences will yield a z of 0.6859 and a correlation difference of 0.04.

BASIC Code[5]

```
10 DIM R(50), N(50), Z(50), W(50)
15 COLOR 2
20 CLS
30 PRINT:PRINT:PRINT
40 PRINT TAB(15); "1. HIERARCHICAL MULTIPLE REGRESSION":PRINT
50 PRINT TAB(15); "2. INTERACTION ANALYSIS WITH ONE PRODUCT
   TERM":PRINT
60 PRINT TAB(15); "3. INTERACTION ANALYSIS FOR THREE-WAY PRODUCT
   TERM":PRINT
70 PRINT TAB(15); "4. INTERACTION ANALYSIS WITH QUADRATIC
   EFFECTS":PRINT
80 PRINT TAB(15); "5. TEST OF DIFFERENCE FOR INDEPENDENT
   CORRELATIONS":PRINT
90 PRINT TAB(15); "6. TEST OF DIFFERENCE FOR DEPENDENT
   CORRELATIONS":PRINT
100 PRINT TAB(15); "7. QUIT":PRINT:PRINT
110 PRINT TAB(15); "ENTER THE NUMBER OF THE OPTION YOU WANT:";
120 INPUT " ", C
130 IF C = 1 THEN GOTO 200
140 IF C = 2 THEN GOTO 390
150 IF C = 3 THEN GOTO 700
160 IF C = 4 THEN GOTO 1170
170 IF C = 5 THEN GOTO 1560
180 IF C = 6 THEN GOTO 1880
190 IF C > 6 THEN GOTO 2170
200 CLS
210 PRINT TAB(18); "HIERARCHICAL MULTIPLE REGRESSION
   ANALYSIS"
220 PRINT:PRINT:PRINT
230 INPUT "ENTER THE MULTIPLE R FOR THE ORIGINAL EQUATION:",
   R1:PRINT
240 INPUT "ENTER THE NUMBER OF PREDICTORS IN THE ORIGINAL
   EQUATION:", K1:PRINT
```

```
250 INPUT  "ENTER THE MULTIPLE R FOR THE EXPANDED
    EQUATION:", R2:PRINT
260 INPUT  "ENTER THE NUMBER OF PREDICTORS IN THE
    EXPANDED EQUATION:", K2:PRINT
270 INPUT  "ENTER THE TOTAL SAMPLE SIZE: ", N:PRINT
280 DIFF = (R2 * R2) – (R1 * R1)
290 DEM1 = DIFF / (K2 – K1)
300 DEM2 = (1 – (R2 * R2)) / (N – K2 – 1)
310 F1 = DEM1 / DEM2
320 DF1 = K2 – K1
330 DF2 = N – K2 – 1
340 PRINT  "INCREMENT IN R SQUARE BY USING THE EXPANDED
    EQUATION:";DIFF:PRINT
350 PRINT  "F FOR INCREMENT:";F1; "WITH DF =";DF1; ",";DF2: PRINT:PRINT
360 PRINT :INPUT  "PRESS 1 FOR ANOTHER HIERARCHICAL
    ANALYSIS, 2 FOR INDEX:", C
370 IF C = 1 THEN GOTO 200
380 GOTO 20
390 CLS
400 PRINT TAB(10); "TWO PREDICTOR ANALYSIS FOR EVALUATING THE
    SLOPE OF Y ON X1"
410 PRINT TAB(23); "AT A PARTICULAR VALUE OF X2":PRINT:PRINT
420 PRINT  "THE MODEL IS:Y = a + b1 X1 + b2 X2 + b3 X1 X2 ": PRINT:PRINT ""
440 INPUT  "ENTER THE VALUE OF a:", A:PRINT
450 INPUT  "ENTER THE VALUE OF b1:", B1:PRINT
460 INPUT  "ENTER THE VALUE OF b2:", B2:PRINT
470 INPUT  "ENTER THE VALUE OF b3:", B3:PRINT
480 INPUT  "ENTER THE TOTAL SAMPLE SIZE:", N:PRINT
490 INPUT  "ENTER THE VARIANCE OF b1:", VB1:PRINT
500 INPUT  "ENTER THE VARIANCE OF b3:", VB3:PRINT
510 INPUT  "ENTER THE COVARIANCE OF b1,b3:", COV1:PRINT
515 INPUT  "ENTER THE VALUE OF X2 TO BE EVALUATED:", X2:PRINT
520 K = 3
530 A1 = A + B2 * X2
540 B1X2 = B1 + B3 * X2
550 CC1 = X2 * X2 * VB3
560 CC2 = 2 * X2 * COV1
570 CCC = VB1 + CC1 + CC2
580 CC = SQR(CCC)
590 T = B1X2 / CC
600 DF1 = N – K – 1
610 CLS
620 PRINT:PRINT:PRINT
630 PRINT  "THE INTERCEPT FOR Y ON X1 WHEN X2 = ";X2; "IS:";A1:PRINT
640 PRINT  "THE SLOPE OF Y ON X1 WHEN X2 =";X2; "IS:";B1X2:PRINT
650 PRINT  "THE CORRESPONDING STANDARD ERROR IS:";CC:PRINT
660 PRINT  "THE t =";T; "WITH DF =";DF1:PRINT:PRINT:PRINT
670 INPUT  "PRESS 1 FOR ANOTHER VALUE OF X2, 2 FOR INDEX: ", C
675 CLS
680 IF C = 1 THEN PRINT
685 IF C = 1 THEN GOTO 515
690 GOTO 20
700 CLS
```

710 PRINT TAB(11); "INTERACTION ANALYSIS FOR EVALUATING THE SLOPE
    OF Y ON X1"
720 PRINT TAB(21); "AT PARTICULAR VALUES OF X2 AND X3":PRINT:PRINT
730 PRINT "THE MODEL IS:Y = a + b1X1 + b2X2 + b3X3 + b4X1X2 + b5X1X3 +
    b6X2X3 + b7X1X2X3"
740 PRINT:PRINT
770 INPUT "ENTER THE TOTAL SAMPLE SIZE:", N:PRINT
780 INPUT "ENTER THE VALUE OF a:", A:PRINT
790 INPUT "ENTER THE VALUE OF b1:", B1:PRINT
800 INPUT "ENTER THE VALUE OF b2:", B2:PRINT
810 INPUT "ENTER THE VALUE OF b3:", B3:PRINT
820 INPUT "ENTER THE VALUE OF b4:", B4:PRINT
830 INPUT "ENTER THE VALUE OF b5:", B5:PRINT
840 INPUT "ENTER THE VALUE OF b6:", B6:PRINT
850 INPUT "ENTER THE VALUE OF b7:", B7:PRINT
860 INPUT "ENTER THE VARIANCE OF b1:", VB1:PRINT
870 INPUT "ENTER THE VARIANCE OF b4:", VB4:PRINT
880 INPUT "ENTER THE VARIANCE OF b5:", VB5:PRINT
890 INPUT "ENTER THE VARIANCE OF b7:", VB7:PRINT
900 INPUT "ENTER THE COVARIANCE OF b1,b4:", COV1:PRINT
910 INPUT "ENTER THE COVARIANCE OF b1,b5:", COV2:PRINT
920 INPUT "ENTER THE COVARIANCE OF b1,b7:", COV3:PRINT
930 INPUT "ENTER THE COVARIANCE OF b4,b5:", COV4:PRINT
940 INPUT "ENTER THE COVARIANCE OF b4,b7:", COV5:PRINT
950 INPUT "ENTER THE COVARIANCE OF b5,b7:", COV6:PRINT
955 INPUT "ENTER A PARTICULAR VALUE OF X2:", X2:PRINT
960 INPUT "ENTER A PARTICULAR VALUE OF X3:", X3:PRINT
965 K = 7
970 AX2X3 = A + B2 * X2 + B3 * X3 + B6 * X2 * X3
980 B1X2X3 = B1 + B4 * X2 + B5 * X3 + B7 * X2 * X3
990 CC1 = VB1 + X2 * X2 * VB4 + X3 * X3 * VB5 + X2 * X2 * X3 * X3 * VB7
1000 CC2 = 2 * X2 * COV1 + 2 * X3 * COV2 + 2 * X2 * X3 * COV4 + 2 * X2 * X3
    * COV3
1010 CC3 = 2 * X2 * X2 * X3 * COV5 + 2 * X2 * X3 * X3 * COV6
1020 CCC – CC1 + CC2 ı CC3
1030 CC = SQR(CCC)
1040 T = B1X2X3 / CC
1050 DF1 = N – K – 1
1060 CLS
1070 PRINT:PRINT:PRINT
1080 PRINT "THE INTERCEPT OF Y ON X1 WHEN X2, X3 =";X2; ",";X3;
    "IS:";AX2X3
1090 PRINT
1100 PRINT "THE SLOPE OF Y ON X1 WHEN X2, X3 = ";X2; ",";X3;
    "IS:";B1X2X3
1110 PRINT
1120 PRINT "THE CORRESPONDING STANDARD ERROR IS:";CC:PRINT
1130 PRINT "THE t =";T; "WITH DF =";DF1:PRINT:PRINT:PRINT
1140 INPUT "PRESS 1 FOR ANOTHER VALUE OF X2, X3; 2 FOR INDEX:", C
1142 CLS
1145 IF C = 1 THEN PRINT
1150 IF C = 1 THEN GOTO 955
1160 GOTO 20
1170 CLS

```
1180 PRINT TAB(14); "INTERACTION ANALYSIS FOR EVALUATING THE
     SLOPE OF Y ON X1"
1190 PRINT TAB(15); "AT A PARTICULAR VALUE OF X2 FOR MODELS WITH
     POWER TERMS"
1200 PRINT:PRINT
1210 PRINT "THE MODEL IS: Y = a + b1 X1 + b2 X2 + b3 X2 X2 + b4 X1 X2 + b5
     X1 X2 X2"
1220 PRINT:PRINT
1240 INPUT "ENTER THE TOTAL SAMPLE SIZE:", N:PRINT
1250 INPUT "ENTER THE VALUE OF a:", A:PRINT
1260 INPUT "ENTER THE VALUE OF b1:", B1:PRINT
1270 INPUT "ENTER THE VALUE OF b2:", B2:PRINT
1280 INPUT "ENTER THE VALUE OF b3:", B3:PRINT
1290 INPUT "ENTER THE VALUE OF b4:", B4:PRINT
1300 INPUT "ENTER THE VALUE OF b5:", B5:PRINT
1310 INPUT "ENTER THE VARIANCE OF b1:", VB1:PRINT
1320 INPUT "ENTER THE VARIANCE OF b4:", VB4:PRINT
1330 INPUT "ENTER THE VARIANCE OF b5:", VB5:PRINT
1340 INPUT "ENTER THE COVARIANCE OF b1,b4:", COV1:PRINT
1350 INPUT "ENTER THE COVARIANCE OF b1,b5:", COV2:PRINT
1360 INPUT "ENTER THE COVARIANCE OF b4,b5:", COV3:PRINT
1365 INPUT "ENTER A PARTICULAR VALUE OF X2 TO BE
     EVALUATED:", L:PRINT
1370 K = 5
1380 A1 = A + B2 * L + B3 * L * L
1390 B1L = B1 + B4 * L + B5 * L * L
1400 CC1 = VB1 + L * L * VB4 + L * L * L * L * VB5
1410 CC2 = 2 * L * COV1 + 2 * L * L * COV2
1420 CC3 = 2 * L * L * L * COV3
1430 CCC = CC1 + CC2 + CC3
1440 CC = SQR(CCC)
1450 T = B1L / CC
1460 DF1 = N - K - 1
1470 CLS
1480 PRINT:PRINT:PRINT
1490 PRINT "THE INTERCEPT OF Y ON X1 WHEN X2 =";L; "IS:";A1:PRINT
1500 PRINT "THE SLOPE OF Y ON X1 WHEN X2 =";L; "IS:";B1L:PRINT
1510 PRINT "THE CORRESPONDING STANDARD ERROR IS:";CC:PRINT
1520 PRINT "THE t =";T; "WITH DF =";DF1:PRINT:PRINT:PRINT
1530 INPUT "PRESS 1 FOR ANOTHER VALUE OF X2, 2 FOR INDEX:", C
1533 CLS
1535 IF C = 1 THEN PRINT
1540 IF C = 1 THEN GOTO 1365
1550 GOTO 20
1560 CLS
1570 PRINT TAB(13); "ANALYSIS OF THE DIFFERENCE BETWEEN INDEPEN-
     DENT CORRELATIONS"
1580 PRINT:PRINT
1590 INPUT "ENTER NUMBER OF CORRELATIONS:", K:PRINT
1600 S1 = 0
1610 FOR I = 1 TO K
1620 PRINT "ENTER THE SAMPLE SIZE FOR CORRELATION NUMBER";I;
1630 INPUT ":", N(I):PRINT
1640 INPUT "ENTER THE CORRELATION:", R(I):PRINT
```

```
1650 Z(I) = (LOG((1 + R(I)) / (1 - R(I)))) * .5
1660 S1 = S1 + (N(I) - 3)
1670 NEXT I
1680 ZZ = O
1690 FOR M = 1 TO K
1700 W(M) = ((N(M) - 3)) / S1
1710 ZZ = ZZ + W(M) * Z(M)
1720 NEXT M
1730 QQ = 0
1740 FOR J = 1 TO K
1750 QQ = QQ + ((N(J) - 3) * (Z(J) - ZZ) * (Z(J) - ZZ))
1760 NEXT J
1770 DF1 = K - 1
1780 CLS
1790 PRINT:PRINT:PRINT
1800 IF DF1 = 1 THEN GOTO 1830
1810 PRINT "CHI SQUARE FOR DIFFERENCE:";QQ; "WITH DF =";DF1
1820 GOTO 1840
1830 PRINT "Z SCORE FOR DIFFERENCE:", SQR(QQ)
1840 PRINT:PRINT:PRINT
1850 INPUT "PRESS 1 FOR ANOTHER TEST OF DIFFERENCE, 2 FOR INDEX:", C
1860 IF C = 1 THEN GOTO 1560
1870 GOTO 20
1880 CLS
1890 PRINT TAB(14); "TEST OF THE DIFFERENCE BETWEEN TWO
     DEPENDENT CORRELATIONS"
1900 PRINT:PRINT
1910 INPUT "ENTER THE SAMPLE SIZE: ", N:PRINT
1920 INPUT "ENTER THE CORRELATION BETWEEN X AT TIME 1 AND X AT
     TIME 2:", R12
1930 PRINT
1940 INPUT "ENTER THE CORRELATION BETWEEN X AT TIME 1 AND Y AT
     TIME 1:", R13
1950 PRINT
1960 INPUT "ENTER THE CORRELATION BETWEEN X AT TIME 1 AND Y AT
     TIME 2:", R14
1970 PRINT
1980 INPUT "ENTER THE CORRELATION BETWEEN X AT TIME 2 AND Y AT
     TIME 1:", R23
1990 PRINT
2000 INPUT "ENTER THE CORRELATION BETWEEN X AT TIME 2 AND Y AT
     TIME 2:", R24
2010 PRINT
2020 INPUT "ENTER THE CORRELATION BETWEEN Y AT TIME 1 AND Y AT
     TIME 2:", R34
2030 C1 = ((R12 - (R23 * R13)) * (R34 - (R24 * R34))) + ((R14 - (R12 * R24)) *
     (R23 - (R12 * R13)))
2040 C2 = (R12 - (R14 * (R24)) * (R34 - (R13 * R14)) + ((R14 - (R13 * R34)) *
     (R23 - (R34 * R24)))
2050 C = C1 + C2
2060 P1 = SQR(N) * (R13 - R24)
2070 PP = ((1 - R14 * R14) * (1 - R14 * R14)) + ((1 - R23 * R23) * (1 - R23 * R23)) - C
2080 P2 = SQR(PP)
2090 Z = P1 / P2
```

```
2100 CLS
2110 PRINT:PRINT:PRINT
2115 PRINT  "DIFFERENCE IN CORRELATIONS:";R13 – R24:PRINT
2120 PRINT  "Z SCORE FOR DIFFERENCE:";Z
2130 PRINT:PRINT:PRINT
2140 INPUT  "PRESS 1 FOR ANOTHER TEST OF DIFFERENCE, 2 FOR INDEX:", C
2150 IF C = 1 THEN GOTO 1880
2160 GOTO 20
2170 CLS
2180 END
```

NOTES

1. When suppressor variables are present, this interpretation of semi-partial correlations is flawed (see Cohen and Cohen, 1983).

2. Technically, the models implied by equations 2.1 and 2.2 are both conditional in nature. For equation 2.1, the focus is on the conditional expectation of $E(Y|X1, X2)$, and for equation 2.2, the focus is on the conditional expectation of $E(Y|X1, X2 = O)$.

3. There are alternative approaches for defining error terms and executing simple main effects analysis (see Kmeta, 1986). Present approach is relatively conservative.

4. Namely, (a) that the residuals in the population are normally distributed, (b) that the *latent* continuous variables are multivariate normally distributed (is it not assumed that the product term is normally distributed), and (c) that a given observed score is a function of a true score and error score, as described by the tenents of classic test theory.

5. In the BASIC code that follows below, every line is assigned a line number. Any line without a line number is a continuation from the previous line and would appear on that line on the computer screen. An IBM compatible copy of the program (in both BASIC and machine code) can be obtained from the first author at a nominal charge to cover cost at the Department of Psychology, SUNYA, Albany, New York, 12222.

REFERENCES

AITKIN, M. A. (1973) "Fixed-width confidence intervals in linear regression with applications to the Johnson-Neyman technique." British Journal of Mathematical and Statistical Psychology 26: 261-269.

AJZEN, I. and FISHBEIN, M. (1980) Understanding Attitudes and Predicting Social Behavior. Englewood Cliffs, NJ: Prentice Hall

ALLIGER, G. (1987) "An equation to simplify correction of range restricted standard deviations and correlations when the population variance is unknown." Educational and Psychological Measurement 47: 615-616.

ALLIGER, G.,and ALEXANDER, A. (1988) The Effects of Compensatory Selection. Unpublished manuscript, State University of New York, Department of Psychology, Albany.

ALLISON, P. D. (1977) "Testing for interaction in multiple regression." American Journal of Sociology 83: 144-153.

ALTHAUSER, R. P. (1971) "Multicollinearity and non-additive regression models," pp. 453-472 in H. M. Blalock, Jr. (ed.) Causal Models in the Social Sciences. Chicago: Aldine-Atherton.

ANDERSON, N. H. (1981) Foundations of Information Integration Theory. New York: Academic Press.

ANDERSON, N. H. (1982) Methods of Information Integration Theory. New York: Academic Press.

ARVEY, R. D., MAXWELL, S., and ABRAHAM, L. (1985) "Reliability artifacts in comparable worth procedures." Journal of Applied Psychology 70: 695-705.

ASHER, H. B. (1976) Causal Modeling. Beverly Hills, CA: Sage.

BERRY, W. D. and FELDMAN, S. (1985) Multiple Regression in Practice. Beverly Hills, CA: Sage

BIRNBAUM, M. H. (1982) "Controversies in psychological measurement," pp. 401-486 in B. Wegner (ed.) Social Attitudes and Psychological Measurement. Hillsdale, NJ: Lawrence Erlbaum.

BLALOCK, H. M. (1979) Social Statistics. New York: McGraw Hill.

BLALOCK, H. M., Jr. (1969) Theory Construction: From Verbal to Mathematical Formulations. Englewood Cliffs, NJ: Prentice-Hall.

BOHRNSTEDT, G. W. and CARTER, T. M. (1971) "Robustness in regression analysis," pp. 118-146 in H. L. Costner (ed.) Sociological Methodology. San Francisco: Jossey-Bass.

BOHRNSTEDT, G. W. and MARWELL, G. (1978) "The reliability of products of two random variables," pp. 254-273 in K. F. Schuessler (ed.) Sociological Methodology. San Francisco: Jossey-Bass.

BOIK, R. J. (1979) "Interactions, partial interactions, and interaction contrasts in the analysis of variance." Psychological Bulletin 86: 1084-1089.

BORGATTA, E. F. and BOHRNSTEDT, G. W. (1980) "Level of measurement: Once over again." Sociological Methods and Research 9: 147-160.

BROGDEN, H. E. and TAYLOR, E. K. (1950) "A theory and classification of criterion bias." Educational and Psychological Measurement 10: 159-186.

BUSEMEYER, J. R. and JONES, L. (1983) "Analysis of multiplicative combination rules when the causal variables are measured with error." Psychological Bulletin 93: 549-562.

CLEARY, T. (1968) "Test bias: Prediction of grades of Negro and white students in integrated colleges." Journal of Educational Measurement 5: 115-124.

COHEN, J. (1978) "Partial products are interactions; partialed products are curve components." Psychological Bulletin 93: 549-562.

COHEN, J. (1988) Statistical Power Analysis for the Behavior Sciences. Hillsdale, NJ: Lawrence Erlbaum.

COHEN, J. and COHEN, P. (1975) Applied Multiple Regression for the Behavioral Sciences. Hillsdale, NJ: Lawrence Erlbaum.

COHEN, J., and COHEN, P. (1983) Applied Multiple Regression for the Behavioral Sciences (2nd ed.). Hillsdale, NJ: Lawrence Erlbaum.

CRAMER, E. M. and APPLEBAUM, M. I. (1980) "Nonorthogonal analysis of variance - Once again." Psychological Bulletin 87: 51-57.

CRONBACH, L. (1987) "Statistical tests for moderator variables: Flaws in analysis recently proposed." Psychological Bulletin 102: 414-417.

CRONBACH, L. J. and GLESER, G. C. (1957) Psychological Tests and Personal Decisions (2nd ed.). Urbana: University of Illinois Press.

CRONBACH, L. J. and SNOW, R. E. (1981) Aptitudes and Instructional Methods: A Handbook for Research on Interactions. New York: Irvington.

DARLINGTON, R. B. (1968) "Multiple regression in psychological research and practice." Psychological Bulletin 69: 161-182.

DRAPER, N. and SMITH, H. (1981) Applied Regression Analysis. New York: Academic Press.

DUNLAP, W. P. and KEMERY, E. (1987) "Failure to detect moderating effects: Is multicollinearity the problem?" Psychological Bulletin 102: 418-420.

ETZION, D. (1984) "Moderating the effects of social support on the stress-burnout relationship." Journal of Applied Psychology 69: 615-622.

EVANS, M. T. (1985) "A Monte Carlo study of the effects of correlated method variance in moderated multiple regression analysis." Organizational Behavior and Human Decision Processes 36: 305-323.

EZEKIEL, M. and FOX, K. A. (1959) Methods of Correlation and Regression Analysis. New York: John Wiley.

FERIS, G. R., BERGIN, T. G., and WAYNE, S. J. (1988) "Personal characteristics, job performance, and absenteeism of public school teachers." Journal of Applied Social Psychology 18: 552-563.

FISHER, G. A. (1988) "Problems in the use and interpretation of product variables," pp. 84-107 in J. Long (ed.) Common Problems/Proper Solutions: Avoiding Error in Quantitative Research. Newbury Park, CA: Sage.

FOLLETTE, V. M. and JACOBSON, N. S. (1987) "Importance of attribution as a predictor of how people cope with failure." Journal of Personality and Social Psychology 52: 1205-1211.

FRIEDRICH, R. (1982) "In defense of multiplicative terms of multiple regression equations." American Journal of Political Science 26: 797-833.

92

FULLER, W. A. and HIDIROGLU, M. A. (1978) "Regression estimation after correction for attenuation." Journal of the American Statistical Association 73: 99-104.

GORDON, R. A. (1968) "Issues in multiple regression." American Journal of Sociology 73: 592-619.

HAYDUK, L. (1987) Structural Equation Modeling with LISREL. Baltimore: Johns Hopkins Press.

HAYDUK, L. and WONNACUTT, T. (1980) "Effect equations or effect coefficients: A note on the visual and verbal presentation of multiple regression interactions." Canadian Journal of Sociology 5: 399-404.

HAYS, W. L. (1983) Statistics. New York: Holt, Rinehart & Winston.

HEDGES, L. V. and OLKIN, I. (1985) Statistical Methods for Meta-analysis. New York: Academic Press.

HEISE, D. R. (1986) "Estimating non-linear models: Correcting for measurement error." Sociological Methods of Research 14: 447-472.

HOLLAND, B. S. and COPENHAVER, M. (1988) "Improved Bonferroni-type multiple testing procedures." Psychological Bulletin 104: 145-149.

HOLM, S. (1979) "A simple sequentially rejective multiple test procedure." Scandinavia Journal of Statistics 6: 65-70.

JACCARD, J., BECKER, M., and WOOD, G. (1984) "Pairwise multiple comparison procedures: A review." Psychological Bulletin 96: 589-596.

JACCARD, J. and DITTUS, P. (1990) "Idiographic and nomothetic perspectives on research methods and data analysis," pp. 312-351 in C. Hendrick and M. Clark (eds.) Research Methods in Personality and Social Psychology. Newbury Park, CA: Sage.

JOHNSON, P. O. and FAY, L. C. (1950) "The Johnson-Neyman technique, its theory and application." Psychometrika 15: 349-367.

JOHNSON, P. O. and JACKSON, R. (1959) Modern Statistical Methods: Descriptive and Inductive. Chicago: Rand McNally.

JOHNSON, P. O. and NEYMAN, J. (1936) "Tests of certain linear hypotheses and their application to some educational problems." Statistical Research Memoirs 1: 57-93.

JOHNSTON, J. (1972) Econometric Methods. New York: McGraw-Hill.

JÖRESKOG, K. and SÖRBOM, D. (1988) LISREL 7: A Guide to the Program and Applications. Chicago: SPSS.

KENNY, D. (1979) Correlation and Causality. New York: John Wiley.

KENNY, D. A. and JUDD, C. M. (1984) "Estimating the nonlinear and interactive effects of latent variables." Psychological Bulletin 96: 201-210.

KEPPEL, G. (1982) Design and Analysis: A Researcher's Handbook (2nd ed.). Englewood Cliffs, NJ: Prentice-Hall.

KERLINGER, F. N. and PEDHAZUR, E. J. (1973) Multiple Regression in Behavioral Research. New York: Holt, Rinehart & Winston.

KESELMAN, H. (1975) "A Monte Carlo investigation of three estimates of treatment magnitude: Epsilon squared, eta squared, omega squared." Canadian Psychological Review 16: 44-48.

KIM, J. and FERREE. G. (1981) "Standardization in causal analysis." Sociological Methods and Research 10: 22-43.

KMENTA, J. (1986) Elements of Econometrics. New York: Macmillan.

LAROCCO, J., HOUSE, S. and FRENCH, R. (1980) "Social support, occupational stress, and health." Journal of Health and Social Behavior 21: 202-218.

LEWIS-BECK, M. S. (1980) Applied Regression: An Introduction. Beverly Hills, CA: Sage.

LINK, B. (1987) "Understanding labeling effects in the area of mental disorders: An assessment of the effects of expectations of rejection." American Sociological Review 52: 96-112.

MARASCUILO, L. A. and LEVIN, J. R. (1976) "The simultaneous investigation of interaction and nested hypotheses in two-factor analysis of variance designs." American Journal of Research 13: 61-65.

MARSDEN, P. V. (1981) "Conditional effects in regression models," pp. 97-116 in P. V. Marsden (ed.) Linear Models in Social Research. Beverly Hills, CA: Sage.

MARSDEN, P. V. (1983) "On interaction effects involving block variables." Sociological Methods and Research 11: 305-323.

MASON, W., WONG, G., and ENTWISLE, P. (1983) "Contextual analysis through the multi-level linear model." pp. 72-103 in S. Leinhardt (ed.) Sociological Methodology 1983. San Francisco: Jossey-Bass.

MAXWELL, S. and DELANEY, H. D. (1984) "Another look at ANCO versus blocking." Psychological Bulletin 95: 136-147.

McDONALD, R. (1978) "A simple comprehensive model for the analysis of covariance structures." British Journal of Mathematical and Statistical Psychology 31: 59-72.

McDONALD, R. (1985) Factor Analysis and Related Methods. Hillsdale, NJ: Lawrence Erlbaum.

OLDHAM, G. R. and FRIED, Y. (1987) "Employee reactions to workplace characteristics." Journal of Applied Psychology 72: 75-80.

OVERALL, J. E., LEE, D. M., and HORNICK, C. W. (1981) "Comparisons of two strategies for analyses of variance in nonorthogonal decisions." Psychological Bulletin 90: 367-375.

PEDHAZUR, E. J. (1982) Multiple Regression in Behavioral Research. New York: Holt, Rinehart & Winston.

PHILLIPS, J. S. and FREEDMAN, S. M. (1985) "Contingent pay and intrinsic task interest: Moderating the effects of work values." Journal of Applied Psychology 70: 306-313.

POTTHOFF, R. F. (1964) "On the Johnson-Neyman technique and some extensions thereof." Psychometrika 29: 241-256.

ROTHMAN, K. (1974) "Synergy and antagonism in cause-effect relationships." American Journal of Epidemiology 99: 385-388.

SCHROEDER, L. D., SJOQUIST, D. L. and STEPHAN, P. (1986) Understanding Regression Analysis: An Introductory Guide. Beverly Hills, CA: Sage.

SMITH, W. and SASAKI, M. S. (1979) "Decreasing multicollinearity: A method for models with multiplicative functions." Sociological Methods and Research 8: 35-56.

SÖRBOM, D. (1974) "A general method for studying differences in factor means and factor structures between groups," British Journal of Mathematical and Statistical Psychology 27: 229-239.

SOUTHWOOD, E. (1978) "Substantive theory and statistical interaction: Five models." American Journal of Sociology 83: 1154-1203.

STOLZENBERG, R. (1980) "The measurement and decomposition of causal effects in non-linear and non-additive models." pp. 459-488 in K. Schuessler (ed.) Sociological Methodology. San Francisco: Jossey-Bass.

TATE, R. L. (1984) "Limitations of centering for interactive models." Sociological Methods and Research 13: 251-271.

TOWNSEND, J. and ASHBY, F. (1984) "Measurement scales and statistics: The misconception misconceived." Psychological Bulletin 96: 394-401.

WALKER, H. and LEV, J. (1953) Statistical Inference. New York: Holt, Rinehart & Winston.

WEGENAR, B. (1982) Social Attitudes and Psychological Measurement. Hillsdale, NJ: Lawrence Erlbaum.

WRIGHT, G. C., Jr. (1976) "Linear models for evaluating conditional relationships." American Journal of Political Science 20: 349-373.

WUNDERLICH, K. W. and BORICH, G. D. "Determining interactions and regions of significance for curvilinear regressions." Educational and Psychological Measurement 33: 202-232.

ZIKA, S. and CHAMBERLIN, K. (1987) "Relation of hassles and personality to subjective well-being." Journal of Personality and Social Psychology 53: 155-162.

ABOUT THE AUTHORS

JAMES JACCARD is Professor of Psychology at the University at Albany, State University of New York. He received his Ph.D. in 1976 from the University of Illinois, Urbana. He is the Director for the Center for Applied Psychological Research. His research involves the application of attitude theory and decision theory to social problems, with particular emphasis in the area of family structure and population dynamics. This includes research on pregnancy resolution decisions in teenagers, decisions to continue infertility treatment, birth control decisions, and family decision making. He is the author of Statistics for the Behavioral Sciences *and has published numerous articles on applied statistical issues.*

ROBERT TURRISI is Director of the Alcohol and Driving Behavior Program in the Center for Applied Psychological Research at the University at Albany, State University of New York. He received his Ph.D. in 1988 from SUNY, Albany. His research focuses on attitude and decision models of drunk driving, with an emphasis on developing prevention and education programs. He is currently conducting an extensive project on drunk driving in teenagers, a program of research that will ultimately yield a high school curriculum for addressing the problem of drunk driving.

CHOI K. WAN is a Senior Researcher in the Center for Applied Psychological Research at the University at Albany, State University of New York. He received his Ph.D. in 1987 from SUNY, Albany. His research has focused partly on cross-cultural applications of attitude\decision theory and partly on decision theory as applied to health psychology. In addition, he has conducted considerable research in the area of behavioral medicine, with specific emphasis on the concept of social support. He is currently applying meta-analytic methodology to behavioral medicine and population research.

NOTES